4400

Let Us Worship

Other teaching books from Judson Cornwall:

Let Us Be Holy
Let Us Draw Near
Let Us Praise
Profiles of a Leader

Booklets by the author:
"Freeway Under Construction"
"Give Me/Make Me!"
"The Treasure in Styrofoam Cups"

JUDSON CORNWALL

Let Us Worship

BRIDGE PUBLISHING, INC.

Publishers of:

LOGOS • HAVEN • OPEN SCROLL

LET US WORSHIP
Copyright © 1983 by Judson Cornwall, Th.D.
All rights reserved
Printed in the United States of America
Library of Congress Catalog Card Number: 82-74089
International Standard Book Number: 0-88270-542-3
Bridge Publishing, Inc., So. Plainfield, New Jersey 07080

TO CHARLOTTE BAKER,
a fellow-worshipper of God, a co-laborer in the ministry,
an innovator of fresh ways to worship the Lord, and a
long-time personal friend.

ACKNOWLEDGMENTS

Since this is my thirteenth book, my wife has long ago become accustomed to the separation and subtle changes in my behavior when I accept the challenge of "just one more book." I, however, do not want to take for granted her graceful acceptance of these things. I thank my wife, Eleanor, for her encouragement to me during the seven years that I have carried this book unwritten in my spirit, and during the months that I have sought to reduce my thoughts to printed words.

I have never had less personal involvement in the mechanical end of writing a book than this book, for the very week that I began writing *Let Us Worship*, Pat Parrish came to Fountain Gate as my personal secretary. Since I was on a conference tour at the time, it fell her lot to learn on her own our office routine and the idiosyncrasies of my word processor. Then chapter after chapter of this book began to arrive by mail. She edited them, entered them into the computer, and had them ready for my rewrite on my short visits home. She has done an admirable job with great cheerfulness. Her arrival was surely timed of the Lord. It appears that God has joined a team together for the writing of many books to come.

PREFACE

It has been over ten years since a forceful prophetic word over me declared that God had called me to be a worshipper. Since that life-changing experience in a camp meeting in Seattle, I have been used of God to bring many hundreds of people into praise. But this has never seemed to satisfy my deep inner craving after God. As my own responses Godward deepened and matured, I began to minister more on worship than on praise, and the publishing house that released my first book, *Let Us Praise*, urged me to write a book on worship. I agreed with great joy, but every time I would begin the chore, the Spirit within me would either say that I was not ready to write such a book or that the Body of Christ was not yet ready to receive a book on worship.

For seven years I carried this yearning inside of me. I gathered material from many sources. I wrote magazine articles on worship for a variety of Christian publications, and I toured the world preaching exclusively on worship. It was not until the summer of 1982 that the Holy Spirit released me to put into book form the truths that had been burning deep within me for so long.

While awaiting the release for writing this book, I was challenged to write ten other books that I can see, in retrospect, laid the groundwork necessary to prepare hearts to embrace this book on worship.

When the Spirit released me to write this book, I felt that He was instructing me to use the style of writing that I had used for an earlier book, that is, short chapters written so that they can be read on their own, not only as part of the book. I trust that this is as pleasing to the readers of this book as it seemed to be to those who have read *Unfeigned Faith.*

I have not attempted to do a thorough exposition of all Bible passages that deal with worship. I have instead sought to inspire, direct, and channel the responses of the reader into worship, and to share from my experiences and observations over the past few years. If this book succeeds in inspiring worship in even a few persons, it will have been worth the enjoyable time I have spent in writing it.

CONTENTS

<table>
<tr><td>CHAPTER

1</td><td>THE
CALL TO
WORSHIP</td></tr>
</table>

It was one of those gorgeous fall days with a clear blue sky and crisp clean air that makes the New England states such a delightful place to visit. A Christian friend was driving me from the hospitality of his home in the foothills of Maryland into Washington, D.C., where I was to speak at a conference. Sitting in the back seat and enjoying the morning scenery, I was startled to see what appeared to be a large turkey farm in a corn field. As I was about to remark on it, I realized that what I was seeing were not turkeys but hundreds of Canadian geese.

My host explained to me that modern methods of harvesting leave much grain in the fields and these Canadian honkers had stopped by on their migration south to take advantage of a free feast.

Seeing this field almost blackened with feeding geese reminded me of the many times I had stood gazing into the heavens watching the giant "V" formations of geese responding to an inner urge to fly south in the fall and north in the spring. For those who scoff at miracles let them explain, if they can, what mysterious, unseen force of nature triggers twice a year the migratory instinct in thousands of these geese. For the young gosling it is a call to a totally new adventure into a vast, uncharted expanse of sky. For the mature goose it is another exhausting flight of thousands of miles fraught with hazards and hunger. Still, each goose must answer this unseen, unheard and, so far, unexplained call.

Similarly, there are times when Christians sense an invisible yet indisputable calling to draw near to God in worship. For the uninitiated, it is as threatening and challenging as the first migration is to the gosling. The intimate, personal, one-to-one relationship with God is a vast unknown to millions of people in today's generation, and yet the urge to attain it is beginning to surge through Christendom. Though latent and undefined, it is unmistakably there.

For many believers these are days of unrest. In spite of all that God has done in our generation, there is in some an underlying dissatisfaction which is really an anxious anticipation of something new on the horizon. God is moving by His Spirit and we are anxious to know what will happen next. This has created an ideal atmosphere for the religious opportunists. False prophets have arisen amassing millions into their cults. Because of this unrest and craving for the unrevealed, proponents of these so-called "new doctrines" have found eager, gullible audiences. Others, who have insisted that new forms and structure are the only hope for the Church, have had little difficulty in getting adherents. Those who have joined cults, especially young people, have been duped into raising huge sums of money, often at great personal cost, as a substitute satisfaction for an inner craving.

These inner stirrings are so real that they cannot be ignored, yet most of our attempts to satisfy them are futile. Consequently, frustration replaces inspiration and seeking replaces rest. We simply do not recognize that God is causing this unrest. He is drawing us unto Himself.

2

As a boy I enjoyed playing with a horseshoe magnet from a model "T" magneto and using its invisible power on a plate filled with metal filings. These tiny pieces of steel would shiver and quake as the magnet was lowered; then they would crawl over one another as though alive in response to the magnetic attraction. As I would gently move the magnet closer to the plate, the filings would make a chain reaching upward until finally the chain bridged the gap between the filings and the magnet. Upon contact, all of the small pieces would come together by the power of the magnet, and each particle became as magnetic as the magnet itself.

Isn't this descriptive of the Church's present condition? God is drawing His people closer, very much like a magnet. The unrest and uneasiness we feel are merely the response of our spirit to God's presence. Our dissatisfaction with the present status quo is merely a by-product of the attraction of God's nearness. It is not ingratitude that is motivating us to abandon our present positions; it is the magnetism of His person that is precipitating change. The pull is upward and we are powerless to resist.

Some people are greatly threatened by the divine surge that moves upon them; others are excited but confused, while a great many totally misunderstand this drawing power of God and misread it as a craving of their body or soul. But such has been man's problem from antiquity.

Jacob

Didn't Jacob totally misread his encounter with God? Genesis chapter twenty-eight records his awakening dream in which he saw angels ascending and descending upon a ladder stretched from heaven to earth. He also heard the voice of God speaking directly to him. Upon awakening and dedicating the spot as "Bethel" ("House of God") he immediately pledged: "of all that thou shalt give me I will surely give the tenth to thee" (Genesis 28:22). From that day forward Jacob gave himself to the pursuit of material things. Having stolen his brother's birthright and then manipulating his father-in-law's property to his own advantage, he returns to his own land a very wealthy man. With a drive that would be a credit to any corporation president, Jacob had pursued materialism and won.

But God's second intervention into his affairs proved just how wrong he had been. After Jacob wrestled all night with the Angel of the Lord (Genesis 32:24) there was a decided change in him. Physically he was crippled, emotionally he was exhausted, but spiritually he was transformed. He was even given a new name, "Israel," or "the God-ruled man." God's initial revelation had stirred Jacob, but he misread it as a drive to "get ahead." Not until he had ultimately succeeded did he realize that *things* cannot satisfy a longing after God. His spirit had been stirred to worship but his will had directed that conferred energy into the pursuit of "the good life." Yet such pursuit has never satisfied any man, while the pursuit of God ultimately makes "all things" available to the worshipper, for Jesus said, "If ye abide in me, and my words abide in you, ye shall ask what ye will, and it shall be done unto you" (John 15:7). The principle of ". . . Seek ye first the kingdom of God, and His righteousness; and all these things shall be added unto you" (Matthew 6:33) was a divine law long before Jesus proclaimed it.

Moses

Moses was another man who had experienced an encounter with God, although he was far too young to understand it. His preservation from death was ordained of God, as was his being received into the palace of Pharaoh to be raised the son of the king's daughter. This awakened spirit within Moses sent him on a pursuit of social action. He was indignantly resentful of the treatment the Hebrews received and sensed himself to be their deliverer. However, God had not called him to pursue social equality but the divine presence. It was not until Moses took matters into his own hands by murdering an Egyptian oppressor, (Exodus 2:12) thereby necessitating his fleeing for his own life for an additional forty years on the desert, that God could call him unto Himself through the divine appearance at the burning bush (Exodus 3). After this heavenly revelation Moses dedicated himself to the pursuit of God and subsequently became the world's greatest example of a deliverer until Jesus Christ came into the world. Has any one man done more to put down social injustice or to raise his people from slavery to a nation of free men? Yet this was unachievable as long as he pursued it as a substitute for answering the craving of his spirit for fellowship with God. The pull of the magnet was to lift him upward, not to extend him outward. Yet once contact with God was achieved, he affected the life of everyone with whom he came in contact. Through him, God moved upon more than four million people. They were liberated because he was lifted by God's presence. Moses' time in God's presence became Israel's ticket to freedom, but he almost lost it all by misreading the calling of God unto Himself as the calling of his soul for social equality.

Israel

One would think that having this powerful object lesson in front of them day by day would cause the Israelites to yearn to be worshippers. In addition to Moses' life, they had also seen the mighty power of God demonstrated in the plagues upon Egypt and the parting of the Red Sea. Their daily water supply and provision of food was a supernatural miracle, as was their guidance through the wilderness.

Nevertheless, when God finally revealed Himself to them on Mt. Sinai and offered them a personal relationship, they requested that He not speak to them again, and in return pledged to do anything that He requested (Deuteronomy 5:24-27). They traded relationship for law and worship for works. As professional slaves they felt qualified to *do* but unworthy to *be*. They would do His work but not become His worshippers. So God gave them the Law, the Testament, and the Ordinances. He had them construct a tabernacle and form a priesthood. He kept them busy, but it didn't satisfy them. Repeatedly they murmured and complained. They rebelled at God's leaders and fearfully refused to enter the promised land. Their encounter with God had awakened their spirits to worship, but they misinterpreted it as a cry for good works, and only Moses and the Elders enjoyed the presence of God (Exodus 24:1, 9, 10). The rest of that generation was buried in the sands where they had insisted on being slaves instead of sons.

Idolatry

At the urging of Israel, Moses approached God on the

fiery mountain and presented their petition that they be allowed to exchange relationship for service. During the forty days that God was giving Moses the Law and the Commandments the Israelites in the camp reacted to the absence of Moses as though they had totally lost God; they asked Aaron, Moses' brother, to make a visual representation of God for them so that they wouldn't feel so forsaken. Rather than point out that God had not forsaken them but that they had rejected God, Aaron yielded to their pressure and made a golden calf for them to worship (Exodus 32:1-6), and then he proclaimed a feast day for worship. Unfortunately their worship was given to this costly idol instead of to the true and living God. They correctly interpreted their drive to worship, but they prostituted it by giving that worship to something that was not God.

While God was grieved at Moses' involvement in social action as an attempt to satisfy the crying of his spirit, and put up for many years with Jacob's substitution of materialism for worship, and even accepted Israel's trade of service for sonship, God was stirred to a hot anger at Israel's prostitution of worship. Jacob and Moses could be brought to worship, but idolaters are already worshipping. The tragedy is that all of their adoration is going to something or someone other than God. This provokes God to wrath; and when ". . . the great day of His wrath is come . . . who shall be able to stand?" (Revelation 6:17).

James and John

Men and women of the Old Testament were not the only ones to misunderstand God's call to worship; the

New Testament plentifully abounds in similar individuals. For instance, James and John, the sons of Zebedee, enlisted the help of their mother to appeal to Jesus for them to be allowed to sit on His right and left hand in the new kingdom (Matthew 20:20 and Mark 10:35-37). All of their relationship with Jesus had stirred an inner desire which they interpreted as a yearning for power and authority. They felt that governmental control was the ultimate for them while completely overlooking the fact that they had been ordained to "be with Him" (Mark 3:14), not *do* with Him. They had been called to relationship not rulership; to love Him, not lead Him.

Samaritans

Similarly the eighth chapter of Acts tells us that during the revival in Samaria one of the outstanding converts was Simon the sorcerer. Hearing of this great stir in Samaria the apostles in Jerusalem sent Peter and John to assist in conserving the harvest and in maturing believers. Under the ministry of these two disciples the Holy Spirit was conferred to believers through the laying on of hands, and this so excited Simon that he offered the men money if they would give him this power to confer the Holy Spirit upon others (vss. 18-19). Although he had met Christ in conversion, he was unaware of the need for his spirit to worship. Therefore, he thought his greatest need was to do the miraculous. He lusted for power instead of loving the person of Christ.

Likewise the woman of Samaria, confronted by Jesus at Jacob's well, gives us a classic example of misinterpreting the divine call to worship. In John chapter four, Jesus told her that she had gone through five marriages and was living with the sixth man without the sanctity of marriage.

Christ did not condemn her for her many marriages or for her open involvement in adultery. Once she confessed it He ignored it and began to teach her to worship. It is as though He were saying, "You've tried to satisfy the craving of your spirit by your relationships with men, but it is not your soul crying, 'I want a man,' it is your spirit screaming, 'I want God.' The itch in your spirit cannot be scratched in your soul."

Isn't this what Paul was saying when he wrote: "Be not drunk with wine, wherein is excess; but be filled with the Spirit"? Doesn't this suggest that the same thing that drives one man to drink drives another man to God? One translates it as a cry of the appetite while another correctly interprets it as a craving of his spirit after God.

Some years ago while pastoring in Eugene, Oregon where we were involved in a building program, I had a rare evening off. Seated alone in my front room after having a delicious meal, I became aware of a deep longing or a craving for something. Rationalizing that I had not taken time to listen to music for many weeks I put some classical music on the stereo and sat back to relax and enjoy its soothing sounds. But the music only increased my edginess. Thinking that it was the wrong type of music for my mood I changed to gospel music, but its effect upon me was no better. I switched the music off and began to read, assuming that my intellect needed feeding because my involvement in the building program had consumed my reading time. Nevertheless, I couldn't find any type of literature that satisfied me.

Almost absentmindedly, thinking that my craving was for food, I wandered into the kitchen and prepared myself a large sandwich. But inasmuch as I had already stuffed myself on my wife's cooking less than an hour before, I soon realized that my craving was not physical. Finally, I had to admit that my need was not physical, emotional, or intellectual. This left only my spirit; so I got onto my knees to pray and began to touch the presence of God. Total satisfaction swept through my being. All along it had been my spirit yearning to contact God's Spirit, and I had misread it as a craving in my soul or my body. For the rest of the evening any music and any literature was enjoyable, for the deep crying of my spirit had been satisfied in God's presence.

How common this is to all of us. When God draws near to us, His presence begins to affect us as a giant magnet, but we frequently find it difficult to understand. Like Moses, we often get involved in social action, trying to better the lot of others or, like Jacob, we try to satisfy the new drive by amassing "things." We become materialistic in our pursuit instead of letting our spirits pursue God.

Sometimes we're like the Israelites who substituted service for relationship with God. No one can serve like a frustrated Christian who is trying to respond to the callings of God through activity, programs, ministry, or Christian service. The more pronounced the crying of the spirit the more they work, although they should know it won't satisfy their craving.

Occasionally we respond to the callings of God as Aaron helped Israel to respond—in idolatry. We pour out love, adoration, adulation, and a low form of worship on our pastors, our programs, our doctrines, our denominations, or whatever. It isn't satisfying because it isn't God, and our spirit is longing for a fuller relationship with the Spirit of God.

Tragically enough there are always those who turn to

inordinate passion and illicit sex in their attempts to satisfy this inner drive for something more. Just how many lives and ministries have been ruined through this searching for love outside of God and His provisions only God in heaven knows.

While the sin of idolatry and the error of adultery may be obvious to all except those involved in it, the craving for position and authority can hide behind a mask of holy zeal. James and John were not the last beings who yearned for governmental authority more than they yearned for intimate relationship with God. The politics of the Church on earth are too widely known to require explanation. Titles are heady wine to some men and, for them, position is worth any price. But even when they graduate to the top office, their spirits are totally unsatisfied.

Perhaps the most insidious substitute we can make for worship is a lusting for divine power. Like Simon the sorcerer we want to confer spiritual power at will upon the needy or the petitioner. Somehow we feel that displaying His power is the zenith of Christian maturity. All too frequently we draw attention to ourselves rather than draw others to the true source of power. Church history has disclosed that many who have moved in the demonstration of power have also moved away from the divine presence.

Or, is it possible that we fall into the trap that had almost destroyed the woman of Samaria wherein we seek to find in human relationships what can only be found in God. No man can meet a woman's spiritual needs, and the woman has not been born who can meet a man's spiritual needs. Our spirit belongs to God and can only find fulfillment and complete satisfaction in Him.

Sadly enough, all of these substitutes for worship come

from misunderstanding or misinterpreting the craving that God produces in man's spirit when He draws near. The spirit within us seeks release from captivity to soar into the presence of God as surely as the goose seems compelled to respond to the call to migrate. Perhaps since geese do not have the confusing signals of a spirit, soul and body combination as man does, they are freer to merely respond to the call so that their migration is inerrant. But man, in his complexity, often overlooks the reality of his spirit and the entire spirit world and gets terribly confused when God interposes Himself upon mankind. But that's what is happening at this time. God is drawing near to men intending to draw them near to Himself. Jesus Himself stated: "And I, if I be lifted up from the earth, will draw all men unto me" (John 12:32). The Holy Spirit's move of the past years has certainly lifted up and exalted Jesus in a fresh, new way. The outcome of seeing Jesus anew will be determined by each individual's ability to recognize the accompanying call to worship.

But it will take more than mere recognition of a call to worship to make us worshippers, for although the desire may be inherent, the ability to perform what we desire was lost in Adam's fall.

Has God unkindly left an instinct for which there can be no satisfaction, or has God, who issued the call, also made provision for us to answer that call?

THE
PROVISION
OF WORSHIP

The first time I met Eleanor Louise Eaton was when she was assigned as the pianist for my preaching team in my freshman year of Bible college in Southern California. That music was her life was evident from the very first service, for when she played the piano she sparkled and flowed vivaciously, obviously enjoying every minute of it. As these assignments continued, our relationship was enhanced by our mutual love for music, and when that relationship matured to my proposal of marriage I assured her that she would have a piano in the home at all times. The drive for musical expression is sometimes so strong in her that nothing else matters, and when that drive cannot be satisfied, as is so often the case when she travels with me, she becomes somewhat disoriented and even physically ill. This strong musical drive in her needs reasonable access to a piano, guitar, violin, organ, or mandolin, and I have consistently sought to have all of them available to her; not because she demands it, but because she really needs them.

God similarly deals with us! He has never created an inner drive for which He failed to provide a channel of fulfillment. The drive of hunger, for example, is balanced with appetite and the enjoyment we receive by eating. Our sex drives are meant to find fulfillment and satisfaction in marriage, and our need for rest is fulfilled in a night's sleep. God instills a need, and then provides for the satisfaction of that need.

If the call to worship, that seems almost to be an instinct in every human spirit, is God created and has been divinely implanted within us, then we can rightly expect God to also provide an outlet for that urge to worship. At Jacob's well Jesus said: ". . . The hour cometh, and now is, when the true worshippers *shall worship* the Father in spirit and in truth . . ." (John 4:23, italics added). This is not so much a command as it is a commitment. It is a promise of Jesus and a provision of the Father. That we are commanded to praise the Lord is quite clear in the Scriptures, but since worship is fundamentally love responding to love it cannot function out of command; it must be a willing response to a spiritual stimulus. But Jesus assures us that the love that we feel, and the flow of the Holy Spirit that we experience will not frustrate us, but will find their fulfillment when we release them back to God in worship.

"The hour cometh," Jesus said, "when the true worshippers SHALL worship." All other emphases will be set aside for worship. Mere ritual will give way for meaningful worship. This promise follows the earlier pledge that ". . . the water that I shall give him shall be in him a well of water springing up into everlasting life" (John 4:14). J.B. Phillips translates this: "For my gift will become a spring in the man himself, welling up into eternal life." Later in this Gospel John defines this spring, or river, as the gift of the Holy Spirit who would flow out of a person like "rivers of living water" (John 7:38). Jesus promised an inflow into the believer that would become an outflow back to its source, and when the

Spirit flows through us back to God it is worship at a priceless level.

Later in this Gospel of John, Jesus expanded this promise in saying: "Howbeit when he, the Spirit of truth, is come, he will guide you into all truth: for he shall not speak of himself; but whatsoever he shall hear, that shall he speak: and he will shew you things to come. *He shall glorify me*" (John 16:13, 14, italics added). The *Merriam-Webster Dictionary* defines *glorify* as: "to praise to celestial glory . . . to give glory as (in worship)." So Jesus affirmed that the Holy Spirit in the life of the Christian would, indeed, glorify or worship Jesus through us. This is a divine promise with an accompanying provision.

But this is not only a promise of the Son, it is also a provision of the Father, for everything that Jesus promised the Father had to provide—even the very Spirit that would become the key to our worshipping. We cannot lose sight of the fact that in all of life in order for the lesser to bless the greater (worship), the permission of the greater is needed. As in Queen Esther's experience, unless the sceptre is extended we dare not approach the throne.

In the Book of Revelation, praise and worship of God stand second only to the revelation of Jesus Himself. It starts with the worship of the four mighty creatures who are joined by the twenty-four elders and, later, "many angels" (and John's parenthesis suggests that there were about 100 million angels), then a group so large that no one could number them united with them only to be joined later by "all the angels." Promenading through the streets of heaven and ascending higher and higher into the presence of God, praising with a "loud voice," they finally reached the throne room and saw God seated upon His throne. As soon as they saw God this shouting, singing throng lost their speech. The majesty, the glory, the power, and the radiant energy of holiness that emits from God is enough to cause anyone to fall silent in awe. But, ". . . A voice came out of the throne, saying, Praise our God, all ye his servants, and ye that fear him, both small and great" (Revelation 19:5). Is this a command? No, not really. It is a consent. They had been praising and worshipping until they saw God. God simply said, *Don't stop now, children. That's fine; I grant you sovereign permission to worship me.*

When permission to bless was granted, John records that the expressed worship reached such high decibel levels that he was unable to measure or describe it. He just likened it to the sound of many waters, or the voice of many thunders. By simply granting permission, God provided His people with the right to express wonder and adoration in worship, and they responded enthusiastically.

This incident in the final book of the Bible does not stand alone in granting us permission to worship God, for the words "worship," "worshipped" and "worshippers" are recorded over 270 times in the Scriptures. Worship is the *main theme* of the Bible. All of God's creation has been called to worship Him. ". . . Let all the angels of God worship Him," Hebrews 1:6 declares. "All nations whom thou hast made shall come and worship before thee, O Lord; and shall glorify thy name" (Psalm 86:9), the Psalmist declares. God's provision for man to worship Him is consistently expressed throughout the Old Testament as "Exalt ye the Lord our God, and worship at his footstool; for He is holy" (Psalm 99:5). Again, it is less a command than it is a provision for a deep-seated human drive that can only be fully satisfied in worship.

The provision God has made that allows man, the

lesser, to worship God, the greater, could never be implemented by man if God had not made a further provision that would lift mankind from the dregs of sin and restore him to fellowship with a Holy God, for only the forgiven one can step from dread and fear of God to worship and adoration of Him. True worship is possible only on the basis of the divine atonement that was provided by God at Calvary. Through the self-offering of God in the Son, the believer now stands in a personal relation of sonship to God on the basis of a new birth. Prayer, then, ceases being merely a pleading for mercy and becomes the praising of our merciful God. Through His High Priestly office, Christ enables men to offer acceptable worship unto God. Our restoration becomes the basis of our rejoicing, and Christ's finished work becomes the foundation of our worship. As the *Zondervan Pictorial Encyclopedia* reminds us, "The roots of Biblical worship are to be found, not in human emotions, but in the divinely established relationship of God to man." This does not deny that human emotions and reactions are involved in worship, but they are not the controlling factors.

The emotions of man do not constitute the true essence of worship. Rather, it is the renewed relationship with God that forms the basis of our loving response to God. No longer is our reaction to God's presence, "depart from me; for I am a sinful man, O Lord" (Luke 5:8), but like the Shulamite maiden we cry, "draw me, we will run after thee" (Song of Solomon 1:4).

The true essence of worship is when His Spirit bears witness with our spirit, triggering the human spirit to respond in love and adoration to God Almighty. But, hallelujah, He has made that provision.

It becomes obvious to a maturing Christian that the

Christian life is designed for worship. God made us with a desire and a need to worship, and in our new birth He made us able to perform that worship, for when we were born again we received the *life* of Christ that enables us to stand before God.

Paul declared, "therefore if any man be in Christ, he is a new creature: old things are passed away; behold, all things are become new. And all things are of God, who hath reconciled us to himself by Jesus Christ . . ." (2 Corinthians 5:17, 18). When we are made new we are also reconciled to God, and out of this glorious reunion comes the challenge and capacity to worship God in spirit and in truth.

Not only have we received this life of Christ, we have received the *mind of Christ* which enables us to both know and to worship God. Our carnal, natural minds neither know God or the ways of God, "but we have the mind of Christ" (1 Corinthians 2:16).

Furthermore, we receive the Spirit of Christ who enables us to contact God. "The Spirit itself beareth witness with our spirit, that we are the children of God" (Romans 8:16), Paul declares. Worship is fundamentally God's Spirit within us contacting the Spirit in the Godhead. God has made a marvelous provision for worship in sending His own Spirit to dwell in our hearts by faith. This indwelling Spirit shares some of the character of God with us in ripening the fruits of love, joy, peace, long-suffering, gentleness, goodness, faith, meekness, and temperance (see Galatians 5:22, 23) so that we can worship in a manner that is more consistent with the way God is worshipped in heaven.

This same indwelling Spirit of God also aids our worship through the operation of the Gifts of the Spirit. In his first Corinthian letter, Paul lists nine special "charismas," as the theologians like to call them, or "special abilities," as Ken Taylor translates the Greek word *pneumatica* in The Living Bible. These nine *gifts* logically divide themselves into three groups of three each enabling us to supernaturally know, do, and say. By action of the gifts of the word of wisdom, the word of knowledge, and the discerning of spirits we can understand things that relate to God and the spirit world where worship transpires. Through the manifestation of the gifts of faith, healings, and miracles the believer is divinely enabled to be an active participant in the works of God, and nothing enhances fellowship quite like doing things together. The last "special ability" in Paul's list (see 1 Corinthians 12:8-10) has to do with speech: prophecy, interpretation, and tongues. Fundamentally, tongues is man's communication with God under divine enablement, while prophecy is God's communication with man under the Spirit's anointing. These gifts become beautiful assets to worship in the life of the believer, for through them we can think with God's thoughts, function in His power, and speak and understand heavenly languages. Little wonder, then, that we are challenged to worship in the Spirit.

Throughout the Bible the beginning of worship lies in the object of worship rather than in the subject: that is, God is both the object and inspiration of our worship. He initiates it, and He enables us to perform it. Any believer can worship, because he can come to the Father in the name of the Son since that Name has been given to all believers. He can worship because the Spirit of God that provides worship is in that believer's life, and his worship is further enhanced because Jesus, seated in the heavens, enables man to offer worship that is acceptable unto God. Christ even made provision for mixing heaven's incense with our incense of worship so that it will have the right fragrance when it gets to the nostrils of the Father (see Revelation 8:3). As the *Zondervan Pictorial Encyclopedia* reminds us, "If worship is a response, it is the response of man to the living God who has made Himself known to man in His words and works." Worship issues from God, is a work of God, and flows through us to God.

Just as I have made provision for the satisfying of my wife's musical drive, so God has more than sufficiently provided all things necessary for fulfilling the implanted need to worship. That provision is in His Word, and that very Word becomes a channel for releasing our worship. He has also provided for worship through the atonement, and helps us release our worship by his Holy Spirit that resides in us.

Out of our new relationship with God our inner drive and desire to worship God can be completely satisfied. But for all this divine provision, men seldom become worshippers until they have had a confrontation with God, a confrontation that rarely occurs where, when or how it is expected.

CHAPTER 3

CONFRONTATION AND WORSHIP

All Christians intend to worship; that's the stuff of which heaven is made. But most Christians put off getting involved in worship unless, or until, they are confronted by the object of their worship and gently led into a response.

Like a boy in love, circling his jalopy around the block his girlfriend lives on, God seeks an opportunity to confront us with His presence to see if we will flee *from* Him in fear, or *to* Him in faith. The confrontation is His; the conduct is ours. How graphically this is portrayed in the drama of the woman at the well in the fourth chapter of the Gospel of John!

She wasn't much to look at, for life had dealt quite harshly with her, and it showed. The beauty of youth that had made her so attractive to men had long ago been spent, and now she was having to live ostracized from the society of the women of Samaria because of the reputation she had acquired in that spending of her life. She had to come to the well at mid-morning, long after the other women had drawn their households' daily supply of water. Hers was a lonely life, but since she could not change the causes of her social ostracism, it was equally impossible to alter the effects; she simply had to cope with it.

The sight of a weary, solitary, young man seated on the edge of the well was unusual for noontime. His tunic indicated that he was a Jew, and the obvious exhaustion etched on His face, plus the dust on His robe, suggested that He had been traveling for quite some time. As she lowered her bucket on the long rope kept coiled by the well, the stranger softly asked for a drink of water.

Surprisingly, her reaction was instantly defensive. Yet the request was a common one. Very common. She had drawn water for countless travelers, children, and even for thirsty animals. Why, then, did this request so disturb her? Why did she hear herself so challengingly respond, "What! You, a Jew, ask a drink of me, a Samaritan woman?" (John 4:9, NEB). Surely He should know that Jews have no dealings with Samaritans!

Was it His gentleness that threatened her? She didn't meet much gentleness in the course of a day. Or was it those piercing eyes that seemed to look right through her? What was there about this man that made her so uncomfortable? She knew men, and how to respond to them, but in all of her life she couldn't remember having been so challenged by a man whose only request was so simple and uncomplicated.

Jesus' response to the woman of Samaria only heightened her frustration with Him. "If only you knew what God gives," he said, "and who it is that is asking you for a drink, you would have asked Him, and He would have given you living water" (John 4:10, NEB).

Even a casual reading of this fourth chapter of John, in any translation, will reveal that Christ had deliberately set up this confrontation to ultimately change this woman. The subsequent revelation of who He really was prepared this woman to deal with what she had become and to inspire her to accept change.

Haven't we all discovered that Christ still waits at some busy spot in our life intending to reveal Himself to us? It may not be during our morning devotions, or at evensong. It could well be at high noon, when our mind is totally concerned with natural things, that Christ invades our consciousness with a sense of His presence. It is very natural for us to live the majority of our life without an awareness of God, for we are earthbound creatures, locked in a time-space dimension, who live most of our lives attuned to our five senses. Somehow, God and the spiritual realm do not fit into sensory comprehension and awareness, unless there comes a stimulus from outside of ourselves.

Sometime ago, while waiting for my flight out of Will Rogers Airport in Oklahoma City, Oklahoma, I glanced through the local newspaper and saw this *Prayer for Today* on the editorial page:

I can never tell, O God, when suddenly Thou wilt break into my life. Just when I think I am safest, there's a sunset-touch, a flower-bell, someone's death, and there Thou art, looking deep within my soul. For thy faithfulness I give thanks. Amen.

Sometimes God's confrontations are comforting, especially during periods of loneliness or great sorrow. But more frequently, His sudden invasion into our tiny world creates deep inner conflicts. Even an infinitesimally small amount of His nature that is manifested in a confrontation acts like a full-length mirror reflecting the tremendous imperfections of our nature. Who wants to be around total perfection? What woman ever wants to go to a party where America's most beautiful woman is the guest of honor? Or what man wants to walk the beach side by side with Mr. Muscleman, U.S.A.?

It is the comparison of our nature with Christ's that so ruthlessly reveals our flaws. It isn't always what He says, but the attitude He manifests that silently, but completely, reveals our attitudes for what they are. The selfishness that motivates us most of the time is completely unmasked in the light of His selfgiving. No wonder we squirm so uncomfortably while His purity amplifies our impurity and His attitudes condemn ours! The contrast is never complimentary to us. We always end up looking like "the bad guy." Even Isaiah, the most spiritual man of his generation, was shocked at seeing himself in the light of God's presence. ". . . Woe is me!" he cried, "for I am undone; because I am a man of unclean lips, . . . for mine eyes have seen the King, the Lord of hosts" (Isaiah 6:5). Later in his book he wrote: "But we are all as an unclean thing, and all our righteousnesses are as filthy rags" (Isaiah 64:6).

Unfortunately, few of us can so meekly admit our condition. Rather than confession, Divine confrontation usually invokes conflict. We tend to become defensive trying to turn the attention away from ourselves. This is evident in the four separate defensive responses of the woman of Samaria to Jesus.

First, in verse seven of John, chapter four, Jesus merely asked for a drink of water, but rather than provide it, or deny the request, the woman asked for a racial adjustment in saying, ". . . the Jews have no dealings with the Samaritans" (verse 9). Next, in verse ten, Jesus offered her "living water," but she retorted with an argument about the size and origin of the well. In verse fourteen, Jesus obviously wanted to meet her spiritual needs but she countered by suggesting that her natural needs should be met (verse 15). Further, in verse six, Jesus discussed her marriage, but she wanted to discuss His prophetic office (verse 19). No matter what Jesus said, she countered it, attempting either to confuse or totally reject the issue. So do we! But it does not stop the confrontation, for master interrogator that He is, Christ just continues to probe with questions until we see the truth about ourselves.

Her greatest problem seemed to be that she was out of relationship with God, her marriage, and others, and until she could confess this it would have been impossible to make a worshipper out of her, for worship, seat of man's relationship to God, cannot ascend much higher than his relationship with his fellowman. John clearly establishes this in his first epistle: "If a man say, I love God, and hateth his brother, he is a liar: for he that loveth not his brother whom he hath seen, how can he love God whom he hath not seen? And this commandment have we from him, That he who loveth God love his brother also" (1 John 4·20, 21).

Undoubtedly, this is why a fundamental theme of the Holy Spirit is proper relationships. When Paul urged the church at Ephesus to "be filled with the Spirit" (Ephesians 5:18), he immediately taught them to use this new charisma to strengthen and purify their relationships with one another. In verse nineteen he exhorted them to express the overflow of the infilling of the Spirit one to another in melody and song; then, in verse twenty-one, he entreated them to submit one to another. Verse twenty-two called for wives to submit to their husbands, while verse twenty-five asked husbands to submit to Christ, and chapter six directed children to submit to parents, laborers to submit to employers, and for the employers to be rightly related to their employees. All of this is an outgrowth of being "filled with the Spirit."

Is this enjoyable? Do we automatically respond? Of course not! It is as distasteful and difficult for us as it was for the woman at the well of Samaria, or the saints at Ephesus. But it is a Divine imperative. Because the "living water" comes to produce worshippers, and since worship demands a warm, close relationship with God, the Holy Spirit first involves Himself with our improper relationships on a horizontal plane to prepare us for adjustment on the vertical plane. The Spirit will first confront us, then convict us of inequities in all of our interpersonal relationships. If we will confess instead of contest, we will be changed, for that is His ultimate goal.

When God confronts us—when He begins to approach us to be worshippers—there is a tremendous resistance that rises up within us. But this would cease if we could only realize that God does not challenge to produce chaos, but to effect a change. He doesn't come to us to destroy but to build; wise master-builder that He is, He excavates before He lays the foundation. He is not interested in a temporary work, and He takes no short-cuts. Since worship will be the main occupation of the saints throughout all of eternity, He is building for eternity.

Perhaps there are some individuals who reach out and up to God in worship without having to be arrested with a Divine confrontation, but many of the men and women of the Bible had to be confronted by God before they became worshippers of God. Consider the case of Abraham who very likely was as idolatrous as the other inhabitants of Ur of the Chaldees. If God had not spoken to him and called him out of that land, would he ever have been a worshipper of the true and living God?

Moses is another example of a man who had to be confronted before he would become a worshipper. His experience at the burning bush changed Moses for life.

But the burning bush experience was not the result of Moses seeking God; it was God confronting Moses on the backside of the desert.

Perhaps the patriarch Jacob could stand as a prime example of the need for a Divine confrontation. His cheating, tricky nature got and kept him in trouble throughout much of his life. Still, God confronted him at Bethel with the vision of angels ascending and descending upon a ladder that stretched from earth to heaven, and later an angel wrestled with Jacob all night long. It took two confrontations and the better part of a lifetime to make a worshipper out of Jacob, but God succeeded.

Anyone can praise, but he who would be a worshipper needs his own voice from heaven, his own burning bush, wrestling angel, or well-side encounter with Jesus, for confrontation is a necessary prelude to worship. The letter to the Hebrews declares "for he that cometh to God must believe that he is, and that he is a rewarder of them that diligently seek him" (Hebrews 11:6). Intellectual knowledge is not sufficient belief that "He is." It must be a faith that comes out of a vital experience with God. After the experience at the burning bush, Moses never doubted the existence of God, nor did the Samaritan woman need to use theological proof of the existence of God to bring her countrymen to Jesus. One intimate contact with God makes a lifetime believer out of skeptics.

Since worship is the interpersonal relationship between man and God, one of the two must initiate the experience. As we have seen, it is generally God who approaches man, as He did Adam in the garden of Eden. Out of this confrontation will come a new faith in God and a change in the individual who met with God, for when confrontation is responded to rather than resisted, we become

27

more God-like, and this affects our relationship with others, and with our God.

This confrontation will be the initial step that lifts us out of our self-centeredness into a God-consciousness, freeing us from the inhibitions that sin had imposed upon us, thereby releasing us to a rejoicing response to our saving God.

If all of this sounds a bit confusing, be of good cheer, for confusion is the natural by-product of divine confrontation. Just ask the woman at the well.

<table>
<tr>
<td>

C H A P T E R

4

</td>
<td>

CONFUSION AND WORSHIP

</td>
</tr>
</table>

When God confronts us with His presence it often induces confusion, for things are not always as we had imagined them to be. "Confusion is a work of the devil," some respond, while others affirm that confusion cannot be associated with God since the Scripture affirms that "...God is not the author of confusion ..."(1 Corinthians 14:33). That verse is absolutely accurate, for God is not the author of confusion; He's the revealer of our confusion. Let me illustrate this.

In many of the conferences in which I have ministered I have been approached by one or more individuals whose opening remarks have been: "Brother Cornwall, I just want to tell you—," and then they pause while looking me right in the eye and ask, "You *are* Brother Cornwall, aren't you?" When I assure them that I am, indeed, Judson Cornwall on a full-time basis they have often responded by saying, "Well, you sound like him, but to be perfectly honest with you, you don't look like you're supposed to look, and I find it very confusing."

If I ask them what I'm supposed to look like I have been told that they thought I was black, or bald, or tall, or very much older than I appear to be.

Am I the author of the confusion or merely the revealer of it? For a period of time that may have extended over several years as these people had listened to cassettes of my preaching, or they had read my books, they formed a mental image of what they thought I looked like. That image became so real to them that when they were confronted with the real person it so violated their preconceived image as to confuse them.

Isn't this the basis of the confusion that stems from confrontation with God? All of us have preconceptions of what God is like. Much of it we have learned from the hymnbook, some of it came from our Sunday school teachers and pastors, and some ideas we've picked up from religious art and poetry. It is very likely that when we actually meet the Lord in our well-side experience we will find that we have imagined Him to be far different than He really is. God can only be known through His self-revelation. The testimony of a third party may assist, or it may ultimately confuse, but no matter what we may think about God, He is who He has revealed Himself to be in His Word.

It is unlikely that dealing with religion will confuse anyone since it functions within the boundaries of codified doctrine and ritual that can easily be learned by enrolling in a catechism course, but when we begin to deal directly with God confusion is to be expected because, as Isaiah puts it, ". . . My thoughts are not your thoughts, neither are your ways my ways, saith the Lord. For as the heavens are higher than the earth, so are my ways higher than your ways, and my thoughts than your thoughts" (Isaiah 55:8,9).

When I was in grammar school still struggling with fractions and equations, illness of my math teacher necessitated a substitute teacher who happened to be a recent graduate from college. In retrospect, I think he probably wanted to motivate us to a higher appreciation of mathematics, but what he actually did devastated us. In his very first class he propounded a problem in calculus on the front blackboard, and then he began to show us how it could be solved. His calculations filled the entire front blackboard; then he began to fill the blackboard on the side wall. The more he wrote his computations the more confused I became, until I fled from the classroom, book in hand, and ran home in tears to tell my parents that I would never go to school again as long as I lived, because I was a stupid idiot who didn't even know what the teacher was talking about. Yet a few years later, during my high school days, I probably could have stood alongside him and helped him in the computation.

The problem back in grammar school was that the realm of mathematics that the teacher was sharing with me was as high above my head as the heavens are above the earth. He was talking about a world to which I had never been introduced.

God is *not* the author of confusion, but when He talks to us, even in spiritual baby talk, it is so far above our understanding as to produce confusion. Even a prophetic word tends to be above our comprehension, and the many and varied interpretations we have on the Bible indicate that there is very often a mental confusion as to what it means. Even a thorough knowledge of the original languages of the Bible does not always unlock the hidden meanings, for those who knew Greek and Hebrew the best are the ones who crucified Jesus. It is never by the natural mind that we understand God, for ". . . the carnal mind is enmity against God: for it is not subject to the law of God, neither indeed can be" (Romans 8:7); actually, our natural mind gets greatly confused when confronted with the things of God for divine truth can only be spiritually discerned.

Because this is true, God has more difficulty communicating with us than we have in talking to our dog. Humans are mentally qualified, or at least educationally trained, to acquire knowledge by proceeding from the known to the unknown. What we know becomes a platform from which we progress to new knowledge. But what is there in our world that is comparable to heaven? We lack an innate spiritual platform from which we may proceed into spiritual knowledge, since we lack the basis of comparison which is a standard learning tool.

Please remember that confusion is not the enemy of faith, it is a by-product of faith. Until we begin to deal with God on a personal level we will probably not experience confusion, but God, His realm, and even His dealings in our lives can be very confusing to the soulish nature of all of us. Fortunately, it is only our intellect that gets confused; our spirit seems to respond favorably to God's Spirit, even though the communication at that spirit level oftentimes has difficulty filtering down into the intellectual level of our lives. However, we can take courage that this kind of confusion is ample evidence that we must be dealing with God.

True worship will always demand that our vision rise from the earthly to the heavenlies; that our will be in perfect accord with God's will, and that His thoughts replace our thoughts. The more this becomes true in our lives, the less confusion we will have when we are in the presence of God.

After Jesus confronted the Samaritan woman at Jacob's well she, too, became confused and she evidenced her confusion in at least three areas. Since I will be dealing with these in separate chapters, we'll merely look at them at this point.

That worship is the theme of the confrontation between

Jesus and this woman is evidenced by the fact that worship is mentioned ten times in verses 20 through 24. The purpose of the confrontation was to produce worship, but confusion began to reign almost immediately in this woman's mind. Her first confusion concerned the *place of worship*, for she said, "Our fathers worshipped in this mountain; and ye say, that in Jerusalem is the place where men ought to worship" (John 4:20). God in human form was talking to her, and she could only think about a proper place for worship.

She also evidenced confusion as to the *concept of worship*, for she immediately began to plead the historicity of "our fathers," but the way worship was conducted in past generations has little bearing on worship in the present. Certainly Abraham worshipped God, but God was now manifesting Himself to this woman. She, like we, failed to realize that methodology is quite unimportant to God. Motivation is what God looks for, and if our desire is to release our spirit into the presence of God to love and adore Him, our worship will be accepted since worship is that interpersonal involvement of a man or a woman with God. We needn't get confused with the trappings or seek to imitate the proficient worshippers. We should merely find the way that our spirit can pour out unrestrained love to the Father.

Some of us demand full knowledge about worship before we ever begin responding to God. It reminds me of the young man who wanted to read the entire marriage manual before he went out on his first date. He was so over-informed that he became confused and merely muddled his way through the evening, unable to enjoy the company of his companion.

Worship is best learned by worshipping. We learn by

associating with the object of our worship, for He is an excellent teacher.

This woman at the well further evidenced confusion as to the *person of Christ*. He had chosen to reveal Himself to her as the Messiah, but she chose to see Him as one of the prophets. She, as we, lowered Christ's revelation of Himself to something she could accommodate at her level of experience. She preferred to think of Jesus in terms with which she was comfortable rather than to accommodate a new revelation.

Not too unlike her, we can easily prefer to respond to a historic rather than a present person, for we're more comfortable with the impersonal than the intimate Christ. We prefer distance from God to closeness to Him, for the closer to Him we get the greater our initial confusion seems to be.

Not too long ago, I decided it was time for me to progress from a typewriter to a word processing system for my writing ministry. I was strongly advised to purchase a home computer with software for word processing, so I began my search. Initially I was embarrassed to talk with the salespersons because I didn't understand their vocabulary. I tried to smile and say "yes" in the right places, but one salesman put me in my place very quickly by saying that he could tell by the glaze in my eyes that I didn't understand a thing he was telling me. Eventually I worked my way through the confusion and purchased the needed equipment. It took me several months of studying the instruction books and actually working with the equipment before the mystery began to fade and the confusion gave way to understanding. Listening to others only heightened my confusion, but "hands-on" experience brought me out of my confusion.

Similarly, hearing sermons about worshipping, or even reading about worship cannot settle the inner confusion that results from our initial divine confrontation. Only spending time in the presence of the object of our worship can replace confusion with confession.

When Saul of Tarsus was headed for Damascus, intent upon killing the Christians of that city, he was confronted by God in a blinding, bright light, and Saul's initial response was, characteristically, confusion. "Who art thou, Lord?" he asked. God sent him to a private room in the city and left him blinded for a season so that Saul could get to know God through an extended confrontation. Out of this and subsequent times in the presence of God, Paul was able to trade his confusion for a vital confidence that Jesus was the Christ, the Son of the living God. By the time he began writing the epistles of the New Testament, all confusion had vanished and his faith laid hold upon that which he still did not understand, but he was no longer devastated by the unknown in God.

Confusion is more evident in beginners of worship than those who are experienced. Perhaps we would be more accurate in referring to this as *pre-worship confusion*, for once we begin to really worship, confusion is replaced with confidence.

When I finished my flight instruction I signed up with an FAA flight instructor who was authorized to give the flight test prior to the issuance of a private pilot's license. The day I was scheduled to take that flight exam was cloudy. We patiently waited for the clouds to lift, but when late afternoon came and the clouds were as low as ever, the instructor suggested that we make the flight above the clouds. Fifty feet after the plane left the runway we were enveloped in clouds and I was not to see the ground again for two hours. At 2,000 feet we broke through the clouds, so I took my entire flight test with billowy white clouds beneath the plane rather than the earth, with which I had developed a warm familiarity during my flight training.

Twenty minutes into the flight, my instructor asked me if I had any idea where we were. I had carefully plotted the proposed flight, but, since I didn't have visual contact with landmarks, I was using time/speed calculations to try to keep track of our flight on the map on my lap. Hesitantly pointing to the spot on the map over which I thought we were flying I said, "right here."

"Well, that's where you're supposed to be," he said, "but how do you know where you really are?"

I started to explain my calculations to him. "Reverend," he interrupted, "we're not flying on instruments in the clouds; we're flying above the clouds on visual flight rules. Look outside the window and tell me where we are."

"But I can't see the ground, sir," I replied.

"You can see enough of it to plot your course," he said. "This area is mountainous, and the tops of the higher peaks are sticking out all around us. You've looked at them for several months of flying. Now identify them for me."

Looking around, I quickly identified the Twin Sisters and Mount Hood and realized that I had my north and east bearings clearly visible. Before long I was identifying other mountains and the sense of not knowing where I was gave place to a positive awareness of my location. I couldn't see all of the ground, but I could identify enough of the high elevations to know where I was over the ground, and from them I could keep my bearings.

Our coming into worship is not too unlike my flight

examination. Initially we may find confusion hanging over us like low clouds, but if we will have faith in Christ to get us above those clouds we will find great mountain peaks of revelation that we have become comfortable with in the Scriptures that are sticking up far above our confusion level. We can set our course and determine our flight path by keeping these landmarks in constant view.

In confronting us, God will not reveal anything contrary to what we have learned in the Bible. He will merely make abstract truth become personal truth, and He will reveal Jesus as God's Truth personified, worthy of our worship.

Once our confusion gives way to courage we are faced with another potential problem in worship. What is the proper timing of worship?

CHAPTER	THE
5	**TIMING OF**
	WORSHIP

This year I was scheduled to spend the Easter season as the conference speaker in Norwich, England. I purchased my ticket a month in advance, sent my wife to visit her mother in California, and suggested that the pastor slip out of town for a change of pace the week before I was to leave. On Tuesday morning, after I had finished teaching a class at Fountain Gate Bible College, I took myself out for a leisurely lunch, shopped for some Easter cards, washed my car, and slowly made my way back to my office. Cleaning up some final details of my work load, I thought it might be profitable to begin packing my briefcase, so I took my airline tickets out of the file and casually glanced at them. I had already put them in the case before what I had read soaked into my consciousness. Six p.m. TODAY?!! Impossible! I had ordered my tickets for the following day, but a call to my travel agent confirmed that it had become necessary to fly me a day earlier than I had requested. Hadn't I been informed?

I had three hours to pack and get to the airport, which is an hour's drive away. I made it, but it was nerve-wrackingly close! I was prepared to fly to England, but my timing was off.

The best of plans are useless if they are not implemented on the right schedule. Solomon understood this, for he wrote:

> To every thing there is a season, and a time to every purpose under the heaven: A time to be born, and a time to die; a time to plant, and a time to pluck up that which is planted; A time to kill, and a time to heal; a time to break down, and a time to build up; A time to weep, and a time to laugh; a time to mourn, and a time to dance; A time to cast away stones, and a time to gather stones together; a time to embrace, and a time to refrain from embracing; a time to get, and a time to lose; A time to keep, and a time to cast away; A time to rend, and a time to sew; a time to keep silence, and a time to speak; A time to love, and a time to hate; a time of war, and a time of peace. (Ecclesiastes 3:1-8)

This principle is especially applicable to worship. Jesus said, ". . . the hour cometh, and *now is*, when the true worshippers shall worship the Father . . ." (John 4:23, italics added). The time for worship is NOW because the object of our worship is not locked into our time-space dimension; God dwells in an eternal *now!* All of His commandments are effective immediately.

But while we give mental assent to this fact we are habitually oriented to time divisions from years to minutes. Our entire lives are divided into time spans of years, months, days, and hours. Our activities, attitudes, and even our ambitions are catalogued and controlled by our memories of the past, our involvements in the present, and our hopes for the future. Since what we are carnally affects what we do spiritually, it is to be expected, then, that our worship responses will be divided into time segments.

Perhaps our strongest concepts of worship are rooted in the past. Each religious heritage can point historically to times of great worship. The Lutherans point to the days of Martin Luther as days of outstanding worship which became the foundation for their liturgy and litany. The Apostolics point to the great Welsh revival and the Methodists remind us of the days of Wesley. All religious heritages that were birthed in revival have experienced days and even years of vital, viable worship as these believers responded joyfully to the realized presence of a mighty God. While it may be necessary to seek out such history in a used book store, uncensored church history records singing, dancing, shouting, weeping, and even glossolalia as a normal part of the response of the founders of our Christian heritages.

Unfortunately, however, experiences cannot be transmitted genetically, nor can they be transferred historically. It takes similar personal encounters with God to produce like worship responses, and all too frequently it is the doctrine rather than the experience that is passed on to succeeding generations.

Although I have ministered in a great variety of religious heritages, I have yet to find one that lacked some form of worship. When I have asked for an explanation of why certain things were done I have always been referred to their past, although I was frequently told that the act was meaningless to today's generation. This embrace of the forms and ceremonies of the past without present vitality was condemned by Christ when He charged the religious leaders of His day with holding to the traditions of the elders rather than embracing the Word of God (See Matthew 15:6).

We may have an excellent memory of the past, and there is both safety and inspiration in this, but we cannot call this worship, for worship is always a NOW activity. It is a present involvement with God that inspires and releases fresh worship. What God *has* done for us may well inspire praise, but worship, as a response of love to love, functions only in the present.

Some genuinely born-again believers who refuse to lean upon a great heritage as a substitute for worship are so eschatalogically minded that their whole concept of worship is future-oriented. Their theme song could well be:

> When we all get to heaven,
> What a day of rejoicing that will be!
> When we all see Jesus,
> We'll sing and shout the victory.
> (Note: no copyright info., E.E. Hewitt; taken
> from *Melodies of Praise*, Pub: 1957, Gospel Pub.
> House.)

They long for heaven and its pearly gates, and they speak enthusiastically about joining the saints above in adoration of God, but in the here-and-now they are non-participants in true worship. Perhaps their story is revealed in a paraphrase of an old saw: "To praise above with the saints we love, Oh, that will be glory. But to praise below with the saints we know, well, that's another story."

While few of us have difficulty with the concept of future joy and worship around the throne of God, we dare not ignore the statement of Jesus that "the hour . . . now is when the true worshippers shall worship the Father . . ." (John 4:23). Good intentions cannot substitute for godly worship any more than a promise can substitute for a performance. Anticipation of a future response may very well trigger a present response, but it cannot substitute for it.

If, then, worship cannot flow out of the past or be borrowed from the future, it follows that it must function wholly in the present. "Now is the accepted time . . ." (2 Corinthians 6:2), today is the day for worship. We are no longer Old Testament covenant people who awaited the great feast days of Israel so that they could worship; we are New Testament saints and Christ, our lamb, has been sacrificed for us once and for all. Furthermore, Christ has become the great High Priest for all believers and ". . .he ever liveth to make intercession for us" (Hebrews 7:25). We need not await a designated day, a special season, or an inscribed invitation. We have been invited, inspired, and impelled to worship right here and now. While the ordinances of the church may assist our worship they are not prerequisites for it. Gothic arches, well-tuned pipe organs, and robed choirs may inspire awe, but true worship is a response to God and He is available everywhere, at all times, and with or without religious trappings. Therefore, worship should not be merely a Sunday activity; it should be a daily duty. God is no different on Tuesday than He is on Sunday; it is simply that we habitually have a greater awareness of God on Sunday, and worship demands such an awareness. Happy is the Christian who has learned to practice the presence of God, for that person is well on the way to being a *now* worshipper.

During the days of His pilgrimage, Jesus beautifully illustrated this principle of worshipping in the now. Although He had spent eternity with the Father and knew that He would return to the heavens in just a few short years, He maintained a current relationship with the Father. Repeatedly we read of His spending all night in prayer to the Father; not in petition, since He knew that all things had already been delivered into His hands, but in conversation and communion, which form the basis for true worship. His communion with the Father was so constant that at any moment He felt comfortable saying, "Father, I thank Thee that thou hast heard me . . ." (John 11:41).

Similarly, Paul speaks of praying without ceasing, of rejoicing evermore, and of giving thanks in all things. Obviously, Paul did not feel that the Sabbath or the synagogue were necessary for worship. He worshipped on a sinking ship, in a stinking prison, and in a Sanhedrin court. Wherever Paul and God got together, worship followed.

While there is strength in corporate worship, individual worship is both taught and demonstrated throughout the Scriptures. Therefore, since worship is neither an ordinance of the church that requires the services of a minister or the exclusive ministry of the plural body of believers, a Christian can worship morning, noon or night.

Worship that is one-on-one knows no restrictions of place or means. Its only limitation is when, for worship must be offered in the present. But it is human nature to procrastinate. One of satan's most powerful tools is the little word "someday," for with it he can prevent us from acting on our convictions. Just as "someday" will likely keep a sinner forever separated from God, so "someday" will keep a consecrated Christian from becoming a worshipper of God. There is never the "more convenient season" that Felix pled before Paul. If we will not worship today, we will not worship tomorrow. If we cannot rejoice in the midst of trial, it is improbable that we will rejoice in the midst of triumph. If we await the right mood it is unlikely that the right one will ever come along, for all moods have their limitations. But what have convenient seasons, trials or triumphs, or special moods to do with worship anyway? If God is the object of and inspiration for our worship, then His very unchangeableness should make worship a continuously present function. Wasn't it Paul who asked us:

> Who shall separate us from the love of Christ? shall tribulation, or distress, or persecution, or famine, or nakedness, or peril, or sword? . . . I am persuaded that neither death, nor life, nor angels, nor principalities, nor powers, nor things present, nor things to come, nor height, nor depth, nor any other creature, shall be able to separate us from the love of God, which is in Christ Jesus our Lord. (Romans 8:35, 38, 39)

If worship is love responding to love, and if nothing in heaven, on earth, or in hell can separate us from God's love, then surely nothing can separate us from responding to that love. That response is worship.

It is possible to be as prepared to worship as I was prepared to go to England and still miss it unless we realize that worship is an activity for today rather than for tomorrow. Today is all that we have. Yesterday is gone forever, and tomorrow may never arrive, so *today* is the only proper time to worship.

But even if we accept the timing of worship, what do we mean when we say *worship*, for this word means different things to different people. What is the history of the word, and how is it used throughout Scripture?

CHAPTER 6

THE ETYMOLOGY OF WORSHIP

Confrontation with Christ is not our only source of confusion. The use of the English language can also be confusing both to the speaker or writer and to the listener or the reader. Words are not only tools, they can be dangerous tools, for they are capable of concealing as well as revealing. How often I have thought that I had clearly said what was on my mind only to discover that the same series of words generated an entirely different train of thought in my hearers, and I wonder if I will ever get over the shock of an editor's note in the margin of my manuscript asking, "are you certain this is what you mean?" Usually a trip to the dictionary will reveal that I misunderstood the word I had used.

As a case in point, last year my secretary came into my study on Monday and asked me if I meant what I had preached on Sunday in saying that we Christians are running the gauntlet in these days. I assured her that I meant exactly that, so she challenged me to look the word up in the dictionary. To my chagrin, I discovered that for years I have been challenging Christians to run the glove. The word I should have been using was gamut; close, but not close enough to be correct.

I think that many Christians misuse the word *worship* simply because they do not know what it actually means;

they have never traced the etymology of the word or even looked the word up in a dictionary. They have merely appended it to an attitude or action and felt that this sufficiently identified it. But communication demands that both speaker and hearer be in agreement on the meaning of the words that the speaker uses.

The English word *worship* comes from the old English word *weordhscipe* which was later shortened to *worth-ship*. It is concerned with the worthiness, dignity, or merit of a person or, as in the case of idolatry, a thing. In the English court it is still used as a noun in referring to a dignitary as "his worship." Worship, in the verb form, means the paying of homage or respect, and in the religious world the term is used for the reverent devotion, service, or honor, whether public or individual, paid to God.

When writers are choosing between words, striving to use the most descriptive one available, they rely heavily upon synonyms or words that are analogous for the word they are considering, for these unfold varying shades of meaning. Wouldn't the same action help us better understand this word *worship?* The *Merriam-Webster Dictionary* lists the following twelve words as either analogous words for worship or synonyms of worship: adore, admire, dote, esteem, exalt, love, magnify, regard, respect, revere, reverence, and venerate. This is what the English word *worship* means. It is the adoration, veneration, exaltation, and magnification of God. It is when we respect, esteem, love, admire, and even dote on God that we are worshipping Him. Quite obviously, *worship* is totally concerned with the worthiness of God, not the worthiness of the worshipper.

An American visiting England when the Queen rode through the streets of London in her ceremonial coach might be horrified to see thieves, prostitutes, and skid-row bums bowing and curtsying along with the lords and ladies of the land, but an Englishman would understand that it is the dignity of the Queen that is being responded to, not the dignity of the one who is paying the respect.

In establishing and developing language, words are chosen to represent articles, things, attitudes, or actions; hence the performance of worship antedates the word *worship*. Still, that word was used as a symbol of what was being performed at the time that the word was coined.

In the Old Testament the one Hebrew word that is consistently used for the worship of God is *shachah*. It occurs 172 times in the thirty-nine books of the Old Testament. The translators of the King James Version of the Bible have used nine different words or expressions in translating this word, *shachah*, the most frequent one being "worship." But it is also translated as: to bow down, make obeisance, do reverence, fall down, prostrate, stoop, crouch, and beseech humbly.

Quite obviously, then, worship is more than an attitude; it is an attitude expressed, and the magnitude of the attitude determines the measure of the actions. A lukewarm heart cannot perform boiling hot worship, nor can a rebellious life revere God with any depth of sincerity.

This Hebrew word *shachah* was used to describe Abraham's reverent prostration before the three angelic visitors who came as God's messengers to inform Abraham about the planned destruction of Sodom and Gomorrah. As these angels approached Abraham, he prostrated himself completely and then further minis-tered to their needs temporal and social. That is called worship (*shachah*) (see Genesis 18). Later when Abraham sent his servant, Eleazar, to find a bride for his son, the Scripture records, "he worshipped the Lord bowing himself to the earth" (Genesis 24:52), and again the Hebrew word is *shachah*.

This word is used to describe the action of the elders of Israel when Moses brought to them his first report that God was about to deliver them from the bondage of Egypt. We read, "and the people believed: . . . then they bowed their heads and worshipped" (Exodus 4:31). Surely worship should be a natural response to a promise of deliverance from bondage that has totally controlled our lives. Have you ever observed the worship of a person who has been saved from the drug culture? It usually is uninhibited and filled with thanksgiving, for great deliverance often generates great worship!

Every use of the word *shachah* in the Old Testament indicates action. They were doing something as an expression of an inner attitude or feeling, and their body was helping to exhibit their emotions. They not only said something, they did something. They were not merely thankful (an attitude), but they expressed their thanksgiving (an action). They worshipped in a way that they, others, and God knew they were worshipping.

Since the New Testament was written in the Koine Greek used in commerce, rather than in the classical Greek of the scholars, we need not be surprised to find three separate words for worship. The Greek word *latreuo* is used four times, and Robert Young tells us that it means to worship publicly, while W.E. Vine says that it signifies to serve or to render religious service. It is the word that is used in secular literature to describe the service performed by the priests in the temple.

A second Greek word for worship is *sebomai*, which appears in our New Testament eight times. It comes from the root word *sebas* which means to fear, so *sebomai* signifies to fear or to hold in awe. None who has experienced the awesomeness of coming into the divine presence of God will deny the reaction of fear that gave way to reverence and a sense of awe and wonder.

But the most commonly used word for worship in our New Testament is *proskuneo* which is used at least 59 times. It is actually a combination of two separate Greek words: *pros*, which means towards and *kuneo*, which means to kiss. Literally, then, *proskuneo* means "to kiss towards." Some scholars say it means to kiss the hand in admiration, while others say it would better signify to kiss the feet in homage, but didn't the Shulamite maiden find a more kissable place on the body when she cried, "Let him kiss me with the kisses of his mouth, for thy love is better than wine" (Song of Solomon 1:2)?

The word *proskuneo* is far more descriptive than the Hebrew word *shachah*, for to the bowing is added kissing, and this requires close contact. We can bow at a great distance, but kissing requires contact.

To the early church in Ephesus, with its mixture of Jews and Gentiles, Paul wrote, "But now in Christ Jesus ye who sometimes were far off are made nigh by the blood of Christ" (Ephesians 2:13). Unquestionably believers have been brought together, but just as genuinely, we New Testament believers have been brought close to Christ Jesus. If the Old Testament saints tended to gesture to God at a distance, the New Testament saints are beckoned to get close enough to embrace God, to love Him, to kiss Him, to pour out adoration unto Him intimately, and to touch God in deep-seated worship with our senses, our emotions and our wills.

In the story of the Samaritan woman at the well the

communication between her and Christ Jesus contains this Greek word *proskuneo* ten times. Every act and fact of worship recorded by John in the fourth chapter of his gospel is this "kiss toward" concept of worship. It is personal, full of feeling, and fulfilling. It pictures the interplay between two persons who have deep, committed, loving feelings for each other.

Occasionally, before a service, someone will say, "Oh, Brother Cornwall, I wish you could bring us to real worship tonight to where we'll all get out in the aisles and prostrate ourselves before the Lord."

I have no problem with taking a position of humility that brings us to a prone position before God, but isn't it limiting to think that we cannot worship until an entire congregation has assumed a specific bodily posture?

As we have seen, the Greek words for worship contain the element of reverence and respect, but they also contain the added sense of an inward attitude of drawn affection. This is seen in Jesus' response to the questions about worship by the Samaritan woman, who was drawn to Him by His forgiveness and kindness. In John 4, Jesus tells her that the time, place or method of worship is not the important thing, but rather the genuineness of worship. The kind of worship that the Father desires is worship that is done "in spirit and in truth" (John 4:24). In fact, there is only one place in the entire New Testament that refers to a specific outward display in worship in the Church, and that speaks of an act of repentance by a former unbeliever (see 1 Corinthians 14:25). Instead, it seems that for the New Testament believer, worship is the natural outflowing of an inward attitude of drawn affection. God's presence attracts us to Him, and our inner being flows back unto Him in a great variety of ways.

One pastor stated not long ago that his congregation was starving on a diet of Greek roots, and I agree that mere word study for the sake of word study can be less than edifying; still we must remember that the Bible was not written in English, and that translators are often pressed to find a word in English to accurately picture what was meant by the Hebrew or Greek word. Therefore, it generally enlarges our concepts to briefly study the variegated shades of meaning the Hebrew and Greek words convey. In this case, etymologically, worship is a bowing, prostrating, kissing the hands, feet, or lips, and a feeling of awe and devotion while serving the Lord with the whole heart.

The original words for worship in our Bible speak of an attitude being expressed with action. They infer depth of feeling, closeness of partners, and a covenant relationship. Worship is communicated affection between man and God. It involves both motion and emotion, but true worship is far deeper than either of these, and merely uses them as a channel of release for the depth of love and adoration that generates in the heart of the believer who is drawn into the presence of a loving God.

Worship, then, is far more than merely singing a song or clapping the hands. It is an expression of something—but let's leave that for the next chapter.

THE
EXPRESSION
OF WORSHIP

The pastor's role is not always pleasant. From time to time over the years I have had to call one of the men of my congregation into my study to talk to him about his marriage. When I tell him that his wife seems to be absolutely convinced that he has ceased to love her it nearly devastates him. After the shock subsides what usually follows is a verbal protestation of love and an expression of bewilderment as to what could cause his wife to doubt his love for her. It usually boils down to his inability to express his love to her in a meaningful and understandable way. He knows that he is supposed to love his wife, for this is what marriage is all about according to the Bible. But his performance has not been very convincing.

Similarly, most Bible-believing Christians accept that God made man for a purpose, and that purpose is worship. Paul wrote, ". . . we should be to the praise of his glory" (Ephesians 1:12), and that "all things were created by him, and for him" (Colossians 1:16). Life's highest purpose is to be offered up to God in adoration and gratitude—to be true worshippers of God.

What we Christians have difficulty admitting, however, is that most of us do not worship very well. So often our "worship" services consist of the preliminaries, a choral number and a sermon, and all too frequently our public worship degenerates into a formalism that is devoid of vitality and spiritual life, whereas Biblical worship is celebration of God. How long has it been since God was celebrated in your church? Is it a lack of love, or is it a lack of understanding of how to express our worship that keeps our Sunday worship so stilted and stifled?

Some of our frustration in trying to worship may be rooted in the inexplicability, the inexpressibility, and the intangibility of worship. Because it cannot be codified into law or ritual we feel insecure in performing worship. In his book, *An Expository Dictionary of New Testament Words*, W.E. Vine said, "The worship of God is nowhere defined in Scripture. A consideration of the *Greek* verbs shows that it is not confined to praise; broadly it may be regarded as the direct acknowledgment to God of His nature, attributes, ways and claims, whether by the outgoing of the heart in praise and thanksgiving or by deed done in such acknowledgment" (p. 236).

While we may lack a positive definition, we do gain some insight by researching the meaning of the verbs used to tell of worship. The *International Standard Bible Encyclopedia* says, "The total idea of worship, however, both in the Old Testament and New Testament, must be built up, not from the words specifically so translated, but also and chiefly from the whole body of description of worshipful feeling and action, whether of individuals singly and privately, or of larger bodies engaged in the public services of sanctuary, tabernacle, temple, synagogue, upper room or meeting place" (p. 3110).

Since we gain further understanding by looking at the way men worshipped in Bible times, let me review one such occasion. David was old and feeble, and already one of his sons had proclaimed himself as the King of Israel. God's faithful prophet, Nathan, came into David's presence to remind him that he had promised to crown his son, Solomon, as his successor. In response to the prophet's suggestion, for David always heeded the words of the prophets, David arranged to have Solomon proclaimed king. Shortly thereafter David died. Following the period of mourning, the nation gathered to anoint Solomon as their reigning king. In this national celebration there was a time of high worship, and the chronicler lists seven of the acts of worship that were performed by the people on that occasion: (1) they blessed the Lord God; (2) they bowed down their heads; (3) they worshipped (*shachah*); (4) they sacrificed sacrifices unto the Lord; (5) they offered burnt offerings unto the Lord; (6) they did eat and drink before the Lord; and (7) they did it all with great gladness. (See 1 Chronicles 29:20-22).

I used to be disturbed that the Bible does not give us a positive definition of worship, but I have come to believe that we would make an empty ritual of any definition that would have been given. Since the foundation of worship is love poured out it would be most difficult to define anyway, for the moment we encase loving behind a set of hard and fast rules, we ruin it. Spontaneity is vital to the expression of love, both in the natural and in the spiritual.

Perhaps as close a definition of worship as we can find in the Word comes from the lips of Jesus when He said, ". . . thou shalt love the Lord thy God with all thy heart, and with all thy soul, and with all thy mind, and with all thy strength: this is the first commandment. And the second is like, namely this, Thou shalt love thy neighbour as thyself. There is none other commandment greater than these" (Mark 12:30-31). Love that releases all of the heart's adoration, that expresses all of the soul's attitudes, that explains all of the mind's determination, and utilizes all of the strength of the worshipper's body is worship. How weak and feeble our whispered praises are when measured by this standard.

Any Christian who really observed this *all* standard of worshipping God would be branded as a fanatic, and he would likely be banned from attending some churches. But those same actions at a football game would gain him the title of "fan." Celebration of a team's victory calls for a release of the heart, soul, mind and strength, but God is too frequently offered only the "leftovers."

I must admit, however, that the very process of trying to explain worship tends to cheapen it, even as trying to explain how to love generally puts more emphasis on the "make" than on the "love," thereby emphasizing the mechanical rather than the emotional and devotional aspects of loving.

Volumes could be written trying to explain worship but, like the endless volumes now available on loving, ultimately more is learned by doing than by reading.

Not only is there an inexplicability to worship, there is an equal inexpressibility of worship. Since worship is basically the outpouring of inner attitudes to God with a subsequent release of emotional and accompanying expressive body action and a commitment to obedience, we do, indeed, have difficulty expressing it.

There is a passage in the letter to the Romans that my religious heritage consistently interpreted as intercessory prayer, but I wonder if it is not far more involved with worship than intercession. Paul wrote, ". . . the Spirit also helpeth our infirmities: for we know not what we should pray for as we ought: but the Spirit itself maketh intercession for us with groanings which cannot be uttered" (Romans 8:26). It does not seem to me that we need as much help in framing our petitions to God as we do in expressing our deep inner feelings to Him. Furthermore, our greatest infirmities are spiritual, not physical, for we have lived so long in the limitation of our time-space dimension that we have great difficulty seeing into the spiritual world, and we are even quite unknowing about our own spirit. With the aid of the Holy Spirit, who resides in the spirit of the believers, the deep inner love and adoration that we seem humanly unable to release and express to God are poured out to him "with groanings which cannot be uttered." Charles Spurgeon calls this "raptures of ecstasy." What we are unable to release, the Holy Spirit releases in rapturous waves of ecstasy. In this sense, then, we could say that worship is a subjective experience. Its force and flow come from within us.

Worship, of course, is a response to a relationship, therefore, it is not the performance that makes worship, but worship motivates the performance, just as it is not the hugs and kisses that produce the love I have for my darling wife, it is that love that has matured over these forty years that inspires the hugs and kisses.

Worship, I repeat, is love responding to love, so it is not the bowing, the dancing, the clapping and the singing that produce the worship, for at best they can only express that worship, but it is the worship that produces the jubilant responses. True worship may have its times of silence and sighing as well as its times of singing and shouting, but the method of expression does not of itself determine the intensity of the worship.

No matter what form of expression may be used, worship never fully expresses the inner glow we feel when we are drawn close to God. Each could wish that he was three people instead of a mere triunity so that he could express himself in a greater variety of ways. When we begin to worship we realize that our *mouths* are restricted by the vocabularies of our mind, and those vocabularies are limited in the words that adequately express depth of feeling. In worship we also discover that our *bodies* are restricted by existing physical strength and by conventional restraints. Just how long can we dance, or stand, or raise our hands unto the Lord?

Even our tears may be as much evidence of the deep frustration we experience in trying to express our love to God as they are an act of worship. Somehow we can never fully express our worship. Perhaps that is why corporate worship is so valuable. As many individuals express their worship in varying ways, all forms of worship expression can be released unto God at one time, and although no one person has worshipped God completely, the corporate group has completely worshipped God.

That there is an intangibility to worship becomes self-evident to both student and teacher. It is not as definable as the doctrine of salvation or as describable as water baptism, but it is desirable and delightful both to God and to man in spite of its indefiniteness. One thing about worship that is definite, however, is that since worship is a response to God, it requires being in God's presence to perform it. Praise can be taught and practiced as liturgy, but worship cannot. Prayer can be read from a book, but worship cannot. Religious service can be performed in a perfunctory manner, but not worship. Singing can be an acquired art, but worship is not even an art form.

Worship is an interpersonal action between an individual and his or her God when in the divine presence. It is quite intangible. It is unseen, undefined, unscored, and without script, but when it is happening the worshipper knows it, and so does God. Even public worship is merely many individuals responding to God's presence at the same time and in the same place, and often in the same manner, but true worship is always one-on-one: the person and his God.

Perhaps this is why there are far more praisers than there are worshippers. Praise is more tangible, is quickly demonstrable, and easily adapts to corporate situations. But praise is intended to bring us into God's presence while worship is what we do once we get there. We traverse God's courts with praise, but when we are drawn into the holy place with God, worship is the prescribed response.

None of us should allow the inexplicability, the inexpressibility, or the intangibility of worship to deter us from being active worshippers. Love is equally inexpressible, inexplicable, and intangible; yet we enjoy it, and we would find living without it devastating. Worship can be as fulfilling for the spiritual nature as love is for the carnal nature. We can exist without it, but we cannot live very well without it.

We dare not lose sight of the fact that God became man, lived among us, and died for us, not merely to rescue us from hell but to restore us to our Edenic relationship with God Himself. Therefore, the ultimate work of the cross is less an act of rescue and more a work of restoration. Calvary, and the subsequent work of the Spirit in the lives of Calvary's converts, enables us to come back and learn to do once more that which we were created to do in the first place—to worship the Lord in the beauty of holiness; to spend our time in awesome wonder and adoration of God, both feeling it and expressing it. Why have the American churches missed this? We immediately make a worker out of a new convert, while God wants to make a worshippper out of him. Perhaps we have paid too little attention to the words of Jesus in the hour of His temptation in the wilderness. When the devil took Jesus to an elevated spot and showed him the kingdoms of the world and all their glory, he said to Jesus, "All these things will I give thee, if thou wilt fall down and worship me" (Matthew 4:9). Jesus responded by saying, "Get thee hence, Satan: for it is written, Thou shalt worship the Lord thy God, and him only shalt thou serve" (Matthew 4:10). The divine order, recorded in both the Old and New Testaments, is *worship* first, *service* second. "Thou shalt *worship* the Lord thy God, and Him only shalt thou *serve.*" We dare not reverse this divine sequence, for service that substitutes for worship is unacceptable to God, since God never accepts a replacement for anything He has commanded. But service that is an outgrowth and an expression of worship is both accepted and blessed by God.

In suggesting at the beginning of this chapter that worship is celebration, I am not implying that we assemble to exchange emotional highs or to indulge in soulish tumult. But we cannot ignore the fact that the characteristic note of Old Testament worship is exhilaration. David testified, "I was glad when they said unto me, Let us go into the house of the Lord" (Psalm 122:1), and another psalmist exhorted, "Make a joyful noise unto the Lord, all ye lands. Serve the Lord with gladness: come before His presence with singing . . . Enter into His gates with thanksgiving, and into His courts with praise . . ." (Psalm 100:1, 2, 4).

The visual representation of redemption that the sacrificial system afforded often induced a hilarious, joyful, and cheerful response. They watched their substitute die in their place, and when the blood was sprinkled upon them they were assured forgiveness of all their confessed sins. Little wonder, then, that they invoked one another, "O, come, let us sing unto the Lord: let us make a joyful noise to the rock of our salvation. Let us come before his presence with thanksgiving, and make a joyful noise unto him with psalms" (Psalm 95:1, 2). They were involved with far more than mere liturgy; they were experiencing liberation, and they responded by celebrating God quite hilariously. Their minds were filled with God's truth and their spirit overflowed with God's joy. This is a sound basis for worship.

Worship occurs when our spirit contacts God's spirit. The way that we respond to that contact is partially dependent upon our basic nature, and partially controlled by our environment at the moment. Sometimes our house gets very dry during the heat of the summer, producing an ideal situation for the build-up of static electricity. Occasionally when my wife walks across the carpet to greet me she builds up a very positive charge, and when she kisses me, SNAP! A spark of electricity jumps the gap between us. Worship is akin to that. In the midst of praising, something sparks between God and us and, SNAP! We're involved in a worship experience.

As an organist, I have accompanied many soloists through the years. Sometimes, however, I have ended up playing a solo rather than accompanying the singer because as the soloist began to sing unto the Lord, that mystical *snap!* occurred and she found herself in a worship experience right in front of everyone and singing gave place to tears or praise. I have had that happen to me while I was preaching. It seems that I took such a tiny step towards God and enjoyed that bridging spark that brought me together with my God. How easily we forget that God's kingdom isn't multiple light-years away; Jesus taught that the kingdom is here and now. Wherever the King is, the kingdom is also; so when the King is present, His kingdom is also here.

That worship is the total release of our spirit to God's Spirit is true. Perhaps the best way to understand that is to liken it to that mystical something that happens when two people who love each another get close enough to kiss. During his absence he wrote a letter, sent a telegram, wired flowers, and even bought a box of candy. He called to his love as he stepped off the airplane, and all of this was appreciated and received. But when he got close enough for a hug and a kiss, everything else was considered preliminary. This is the main event! Love is flowing; worship is transpiring.

The gifts functioned as elements for the expression of his love but it was the touch, the closeness, and the release of tenderness that made it a loving experience.

If, therefore, elements prepare the way for such a loving experience, are there also elements that prepare the way for worship and which may become the very channels through which worship is released?

8

THE
ELEMENTS
OF WORSHIP

Hezekiah was only twenty-five years old when he took the reins of government after the death of his godless father, Ahaz. Reflecting the godly influence of his tutor, Isaiah, this new king opened the doors of the house of the Lord the very first month after his coronation. Under his father, all temple worship had ceased, and the temple had become a storage building for the king.

First Hezekiah regathered the priesthood and challenged them to reinstitute worship for all Israel and to clean out the house of the Lord. Second, he provided for the recasting of the vessels of the Lord that had been destroyed by Ahaz (see 2 Chronicles 29).

It was not until after all the elements of worship—the brazen altar, the laver of the outer court, the lampstand, the table of shewbread, and the altar of incense of the holy place—had been completely restored in the cleansed and repaired temple that Hezekiah called the congregation together to worship. The chronicler records that:

   . . . When the burnt offering began, the song of the Lord began also with the trumpets, and with the instruments ordained by David King of Israel. And all the congregation worshipped, and the singers sang, and the trumpeters sounded: and all this continued until the burnt offering was finished. And when they had made an end of offering, the king and all that were present with him bowed themselves, and worshipped. Moreover, Hezekiah the king and the princes commanded the Levites to sing praise unto the Lord with the words of David, and of Asaph the seer. And they sang praises with gladness, and they bowed their heads and worshipped. (2 Chronicles 29:27-30)

Hezekiah restored jubilant worship to Israel. But he began by restoring the elements of worship, for he realized that without these channels of worship neither the priests nor the people would have a route of access to God or a means of expressing their worship to God. These elements were not mere rituals, they were channels for the communication of worship unto God. Elements of worship, then, are important.

To review, just what is worship? It is an attitude of heart, a reaching toward God, a pouring out of our total self in thanksgiving, praise, adoration, and love to the God who created us and to Whom we owe everything we have and are. But worship is even more than that.

The worshippers in the Old Testament gave tangible evidence of their heart attitude. They built altars, made offerings, slew animals and later became deeply involved with the elaborate ritual of the tabernacle worship. These saints translated their heart attitudes into *facts* of worship. Even the Magi who came to worship the child Jesus had tangible evidence of their heart attitude in the gifts they presented as they fell down before Him (see Matthew 2:11).

Has Christ's position as the sacrifice slain once and for

all negated these acts that give tangible evidence of our heart's attitude? No! Only the sacrificial system was abolished in Him. Wise men still worship Him, and they will need some elements to help them express that worship. We are being reintroduced to some acts of worship such as clapping of the hands, raising our hands, dancing before the Lord, bowing on our knees, and using our voices to sing and shout His praises; but we have only scratched the surface. A broad dimension of worshipful expressions are just now beginning to resurface in our generation but, actually, they have been a part of worship from antiquity.

Those who have recently been released from extreme formalism and ritualistic worship usually decry the need for elements. "I want to be free to worship the Lord in my own way," they cry. "I don't want to go back into bondage." But it isn't long until they discover that they must either embrace old elements of worship or invent some new ones for, limited beings that we are, we all need something that will inspire us to worship and channel our desires into a true worship experience. The Bible has given us quite a variety of such elements and even Jesus did not condemn them. He did, however, condemn the exaggerated emphasis on ritual practice which was used as a substitute for genuine righteousness (see Mark 7:6).

In the very giving of the Lord's Prayer and the new ritual of the Lord's Supper, Jesus recognized that men need aids to worship. He consistently taught the need for commitment to God, for the expression of divine love back to God, and for purity of heart and mind which would normally find expression in acts of worship. It is the certainty of God within us that gives substance, reality, and power to any external motions used to translate heart attitudes into acts of worship.

God did not make us mystics. When we seek a mystical approach to God we tend to become hyper-spiritual and unduly emotional, trading substance for feeling. Often this approach is embraced for lack of proper understanding of the difference between supernatural and spiritual. Everything that God does is entirely natural to Him and His spiritual kingdom. It only seems supernatural to us because we view all spiritual acts from our natural world. If God never violates His nature in what He does, if all His acts are very natural to Him, then I would expect Him to appreciate worship that is consistent with our born-again nature and that is natural to us. True worship need not violate our God-given nature. It should express it. We need not be "spooky" to be spiritual. The most spiritual men of the Bible were very down-to-earth human beings who had learned how to come into God's presence and worship. Even their great spiritual power did not divest them of their humanity as Paul and Barnabas declared to the people of Lystra when they sought to make gods of the apostles after they healed the cripple who had never walked. Paul and Barnabas "ran in among the people, crying out, and saying, Sirs, why do ye these things? We also are men of like passions with you . . ." (Acts 14:14, 15).

No, we're not mystics; we're men. We're not miniature gods; we're mere people who need to do something to successfully make the transition from our natural kingdom to God's spiritual kingdom.

Those things that we *do* to bridge this gap are elements that help give form and substance to our worship. The Gospels record such elements, Paul manifested them in his life, and the Epistles teach about them and command us to use them, for God has not left worship a total mystery; there are certain things that we can do that both bring us into worship and express that worship unto God.

Prayer is one such element. Jesus regularly used the prayer channel for times of fellowship with His Father, and Paul taught and practiced the use of prayer as a channel for worship. We need to communicate in order to come into communion, and prayer is essentially communication. If we can talk with God, then we can fellowship with Him and flow worship unto Him. Just as nothing strains a marriage faster than a breakdown of communication, nothing will disturb worship more than prayerlessness. How often have we bridged the gap between our world and His through the channel of prayer.

Prayer, in its simplest essence, is a communication from man's spirit to God's Spirit, while worship is communion between these two spirits, and communication greatly aids communion. It is safe to say that the prayerless saint is never a worshipper.

Praise, confession of sin, and confession of faith are also elements of worship. They will be considered in greater depth a little later in this book, but we can't ignore the fact that praise is very often the vocal end of worship, although it cannot become a substitute for it. Furthermore, the very confession of sin is a part of worship, for it is an acknowledgment of the finished work of Christ at Calvary and it is a positive application of divine grace. We dare not let sin keep us out of God's presence when confession of sin will help to bring us into His presence.

Even the confession of our faith can become an element of worship, for faith must be released to be effective, and faith is most normally released in our speech.

Reading the Scriptures can become another channel for worship, for private reading of the Bible for spiritual edification often elevates the reader into a worshipful atmosphere that makes contact with God simple and most natural. Even public reading of the Scriptures can become an element of worship, for this was part of the worship of the early New Testament church. (Private copies of the Word were unavailable to all but the very wealthy.) If prayer and praise are fundamentally our communication with God, then reading the Scripture is basically God's communication with us. Since worship is like dialogue we must have movement in two directions: God comes to man and man goes to God. Like Jacob's ladder, there is an ascending and a descending. If worship is to meet God, we should expect to meet Him in His Word.

Sometime ago I was ministering in a small church in Virginia. That night the worship leader evidenced great exhaustion, and the song service was lifeless. I stepped to the pulpit and offered to take over. Opening my Bible I invited the congregation to turn with me to the first chapter of the book of Hebrews, assuring them that I was not going to preach; I merely wanted everyone to stand and read the chapter in unison with me. At first, every few verses I paused and helped them to realize what they had read, and then we would read on. By the time we had completed chapter 2 that congregation was so conscious of the presence of God that they had already begun to worship. The mere awareness of God's provision for us in Christ Jesus formed that "spark" that bridged the gap between earth and heaven. If the Old Testament priests could minister at the golden altar of incense only if the lampstand was lighted, then we, too, need illumination to aid our worship. Proverbs 6:23 says, "For the commandment is a lamp; and the law is light . . . ," and the Psalmist declares, "The entrance of thy words giveth light . . ." (Psalm 119:130).

Preaching is also an element of worship. The New Testament makes great provision for preaching, for it proclaims God's Word, it declares God's work, and it enlightens, informs, and inspires God's people to respond to Him. Every prophesying and exhortation are elements of worship since they, too, declare the words and works of God and magnify His offices.

Anointed, Bible-centered preaching should be a part of the worship of the church but it should not be a substitute for worship. One notable thing about a New Testament church service must have been that almost everyone came feeling he had the privilege of contributing something to it. Paul wrote, "To sum up, my friends: when you meet for worship each of you contributes a hymn, some instruction, a revelation, an ecstatic utterance or the interpretation of such an utterance" (2 Corinthians 14:26, NEB). Preaching, then, is not the end; it is a means to an end. Worship is the end to be sought in all our church services. Everything should contribute to worship or have no place in our gatherings.

The *Lord's Supper* was instituted as an element of worship. "This do ye, as oft as ye drink it, in remembrance of me," Jesus said (1 Corinthians 11:25). This element of worship replaced not only the Passover but the temple offerings. This is probably why there is so much sacrificial language associated with this sacrament. "This is my body which is broken for you," and "this is my shed blood" all speak of the death of the lamb slain for the sins of the people.

The great beauty of the Lord's Supper is that it is Christological rather than liturgical in the narrower Old Testament sense.

It is not the mere serving of the Communion that becomes an element of worship, but it is the remembering of the covenant we have entered into because of this shed blood, and the memory of Christ Jesus Himself. I have participated in observances of the Lord's Supper that were more funeral services than times of worship. Conversely, I have enjoyed some very bright periods of worship during the serving of the Communion. The difference lies in the concept being presented at the time. When it is Christ-centered there is a great potential for worship, but when it is ceremony-centered, it often becomes a substitute for worship.

Certainly these examples do not exhaust the many elements of worship made available to us throughout the Bible. Space does not permit our discussion of song, Christian fellowship, church construction, testimony, baptism, pageantry, choral presentations, etc., as aids to our worship experience, but we are somewhat familiar with them by virtue of personal experience.

I feel constrained, however, to admit that there can be negatives to the employment of these elements of worship. Each *may* be a part of worship but any and all are vehicles for worship that can give guidance to worship and can become expressions of worship, *but in themselves* they are not worship.

Just as we can have a Communion service without it becoming a worship service, we can pray seven times a day and still not worship. It is even possible for the one who preaches the sermon to fail to worship, since ritual, for ritual's sake, will never produce worship. While it is true that worship does not require vestments, cathedrals or pipe organs, these may be elements that help to bring the saints to worship. Jesus continually emphasized that worship was a one-to-one relationship that was not dependent upon locale or trappings, while all the time refusing to condemn the liturgy of His day. I embrace the statement made in the *International Standard Bible Encyclopedia*, "Anything that really stimulates and expresses the worshipful spirit is a legitimate aid to worship, but never a substitute for it, and is harmful if it displaces it" (page 3112).

Our Quaker brothers and sisters leaned to the mystical approach in worshipping God; so they came together in total silence awaiting the worship experience, but the way into worship is not silence; it is expression. It is not in doing nothing, but in doing something that will stimulate, direct, and then channel our worship unto God. The goal of our life should be to get into the divine presence rather than to find and follow a prescribed ritual. Whatever we find that brings us into that divine presence should be continued until we flow into a full worship experience.

Although varied rituals may help bring us to the place of worship, it will be the expression of correct attitudes that enables us to step from ceremony to Communion. But just what are the correct attitudes of worship and what will be the attitudes of those who observe that worship? And, even more important, what will be the attitude of the One who is being worshipped?

9

THE
ATTITUDE
OF WORSHIP

The Bible does not even give us her name, but she performed a most beautiful act of worship in the house of Simon the Pharisee. Because what she did in worshipping Jesus parallels what Mary, the sister of Lazarus, did to Jesus in the home of Simon the Leper, some believe that this is the same incident. Whether or not there were two separate but similiar incidents, or merely one that has been reported differently by two writers, is unimportant at the moment. Luke merely identifies this woman as "a sinner" who brought an alabaster box of ointment, "and stood at his [Jesus'] feet behind him weeping, and began to wash his feet with tears, and did wipe them with the hairs of her head, and kissed his feet, and anointed them with the ointment" (Luke 7:38).

In this simple story, Luke deals very strongly with the attitudes involved and released in worship: those expressed and released by the worshipper, those expressed and inferred by the spectators, and the expressed attitudes of Jesus who was so lavishly worshipped on this occasion. These, or similiar, attitudes will usually be present when worship is being released to God in an earnest and truthful manner. Whether they produce the worship or are a by-product of the worship may be difficult to determine, but they are active in worship.

The first attitude that seemed to impress Luke was this woman's brokenness, for he records that she "stood at his feet behind him weeping, and began to wash his feet with tears" (Luke 7:38). Brokenness is a good beginning attitude in worship, for tears have a way of cleansing the soul. When we, with all of our imperfections, stand in the presence of the completely perfect Christ, the very contrast is enough to break our hearts.

David understood the place of brokenness in worship, for he wrote, "the sacrifices of God are a broken spirit: a broken and a contrite heart, O God, thou wilt not despise" (Psalm 51:17). In referring to a broken spirit, David uses the Hebrew word *shabor* which means to shiver, to break to pieces, or to reduce. A spirit that trembles in God's presence, or has been broken into multiple pieces, is classified as an acceptable sacrifice in worshipping God. He does not indicate whether the spirit may have been broken by God, by the worshipper, or by the harsh realities of life; he just indicates that no matter what has broken us, that brokenness can be brought to God in sweet surrender, and it is accepted as an attitude of worship.

When David spoke of "a broken heart," however, he used an entirely different Hebrew word, *dakah*, which means to crumble, to beat to pieces, to bruise, to crush, or to humble. To this he adds the expression "a contrite heart." "Contrite" is a word that is used to describe the process of making talcum powder. In days gone by some brands of talcum came in containers on which were printed the words, "this is stone that has been contrited." It simply means that what was once part of a mountain has been ground and pounded so fine that it will float on water. It now has taken an entirely different form. Did the prophet have this in mind when he wrote, "Is not my word . . . like a hammer that breaketh the rock in pieces?" (Jeremiah 23:29).

Worship requires being broken! Most of us have built such protective walls around our emotions that we cannot release tenderness, love and adoration. We're more like the alabaster box than the ointment that was poured out. Until something breaks that rock-hard attitude there can be no love poured out on Christ.

But tears are not only an evidence of being broken and contrited; tears are also an expression of full emotion. Jesus told us, ". . . thou shalt love the Lord thy God with all thy heart, and with all thy soul, and with all thy mind, and with all thy strength . . ." (Mark 12:30). Usually this much concentration and exertion will build such a wave of emotion that it can only be released in tears. As the tension of a beauty pageant reaches the climactic moment when the winner is about to be announced the atmosphere becomes electrifying, and when the winner is announced she generally bursts into a flood of tears as a release of the pent-up emotions that had been building.

Should worship be any different for us? If we, too, have set all of our heart, soul, mind, and strength to come into God's presence, when that climactic moment occurs tears should be a natural expression of the release of joy and happiness. Tears are nothing to be ashamed of, for even great athletes have been seen joyfully weeping after winning an event. Since tears are such a part of our release of high level emotion—and airports, where I spend so much time, are a good place to witness tears as friends and loved ones meet in joyful embrace—we should expect to burst out crying like this worshipping woman, for we have finally come into the presence of a loving God.

A second worshipful attitude that this unknown sinful woman displayed was humility. Luke remembered that she "began to wash his feet with tears, and did wipe them with the hairs of her head . . ." (Luke 7:38). Paul reminded the Corinthian believers that "if a woman have long hair, it is a glory to her: for her hair is given her for a covering" (1 Corinthians 11:15), which suggests two reasons why this act of wiping the feet of Christ was a display of humility. First, in the days of Jesus the women wore a covering over their hair as an outer symbol that they were under the authority or covering of a man. It was not too unlike our custom of wearing a wedding ring. When this unnamed worshipper loosened her long hair allowing it to fall freely around her, she had the attention of every man in the room, for this was an act done only by a wife in the privacy of her bedroom, or by a prostitute as she attempted to turn a trick. The fact that Simon was so amazed that Jesus, with His prophetic insight, would even let this class of woman touch him (see Luke 7:39) suggests that Simon either knew her reputation from past experience, or what she was doing was so classified as part of her trade that all the men were horrified. This woman put her reputation on the line in order to worship Jesus in the manner that she felt He should be worshipped, and so must we. Peer pressure has kept far too many saints from releasing their affection to Christ. There must come a time when the question "what will others think of me" gives place to "what will Jesus think of me?"

Furthermore, I see humility in this act of wiping the dusty feet of Jesus now made muddy with the nearly endless tears that have fallen on them, because Paul declared that a woman's hair is her glory, and this worshipping woman took her glory to wipe up the mess.

Her act indicates her attitude. Absolutely nothing she had was too good for Jesus!

When God was speaking through the prophet Isaiah, He declared, "For thus saith the high and lofty One that inhabiteth eternity, whose name is Holy: I dwell in the high and holy place, with him also that is of a *contrite and humble spirit*, to revive the spirit of the *humble*, and to revive the heart of the *contrite* ones" (Isaiah 57:15, italics added). God declares that He not only dwells with the angels in heaven, but He also dwells with the contrite and humble spirit here on earth. Brokenness and humility form a dwelling place for the Almighty God, and God's presence is a necessary pre-requisite to worship.

Even the New Testament tells us that ". . . God resisteth the proud, and giveth grace to the humble. Humble yourselves therefore under the mighty hand of God, that he may exalt you in due time" (1 Peter 5:5). Pride and humility are not too unlike the positive and negative poles of a magnet. If you attempt to put two magnets together, positive to positive or negative to negative, the combined energies of the magnets will repel and push the magnets away from each other. If, however, you reverse the polarity of one of the magnets and bring the negative pole of one magnet to the positive pole of the other, the combined force in the two magnets will attract each other until it becomes difficult to separate them after they have joined.

If we approach God in the pride of our being, accomplishment, or station in life, we are pushing away from the divine presence. But if we approach God in true humility He draws us unto Himself and none can separate us from the love of God that is in Christ Jesus our Lord. Worship without humility is like love without commitment; it is shallow, emotional and fleeting.

A third attitude of worship that is exemplified in this story is *love*. It was not merely that she felt the love of Jesus or even felt love for Him, but she expressed what she felt. She poured love out in an unashamed, non-sexual manner. She evidenced that love in kissing Christ's feet. Unloving worship is worse than an uncaring stepmother, for love must become the heart of all worship.

Still a fourth attitude that was displayed in this act of worship is *giving*, for she poured out the contents of the alabaster box on the feet of Jesus. That the ointment was precious and costly is indicated by the fact that it was contained in alabaster. Very likely this represented her savings account, for widows and unmarried women rarely trusted their funds to the bankers of their day. Gold coins and costly spices were stored as their savings. In Mark's account of Mary anointing the head of Jesus, the value of the spikenard that she poured out was calculated as a full year's salary. Just how valuable this particular ointment may have been is purely a matter of speculation, for Luke didn't even identify the nature of the ointment. But whatever its value, this woman poured it out on Christ's feet as an act of worship. She gave Him the best that she had. She did not confine herself merely to expressing her emotions; she also gave tangible evidence of her love, devotion and adoration.

I have already stated that one of the characteristics of Old Testament worship was jubilation and joy, but another major facet of Israelite worship was gift-giving. Three times God discussed the compulsory feasts that His covenant people were to attend, and all three times God commanded that "they shall not appear before the Lord empty" (Exodus 23:15, 34:20, and Deuteronomy 16:16). No worshipper could approach God with empty hands, for Old Testament worship involved sacrifices, gifts, and offerings, all of which were brought by the people themselves. No gift, no worship! God made no provision for free-loaders in His economy. They could, if forced by poverty, trap a sparrow or bring a turtledove, but they could not worship empty-handed.

Should New Testament saints do less? The very psalter which formed the hymn book of the early church exhorted the believers:

> O sing unto the Lord a new song . . . bless his name . . . Declare his glory . . . Give unto the Lord . . . give unto the Lord glory and strength. . . . Give unto the Lord the glory due unto his name: bring an offering, and come into his courts. O worship the Lord in the beauty of holiness: fear before him, all the earth.
> (Psalm 96:1-9).

After telling the saints in Corinth about the gifts of the Spirit, the power of love, and the surety of the resurrection, Paul concluded his letter by writing, "Now concerning the collection for the saints, as I have given order to the churches of Galatia, even so do ye. Upon the first day of the week let every one of you lay by him in store, as God hath prospered him, that there be no gatherings when I come" (1 Corinthians 16:1, 2). Nowhere in the New Testament is worship discussed more fully than in this letter, and in the midst of that discussion Paul, too, says we should not come empty-handed.

It certainly is not that heaven is short of funds and needs the meager gifts that we can bring; it is simply that our worship needs an attitude of surrender in giving. We, too, need to pour out our "ointment" upon Christ to release a greater depth of worship upon our God.

Whenever our expressed attitudes of worship are observed by non-worshippers, we can expect them to react with attitudes of criticism. Like Simon the Pharisee, they will criticize Jesus for allowing such lavish worship to come from such sinful people and they will criticize the worshipper for wasting on Jesus what might well have been given to the poor, as the disciples did when Mary anointed Jesus' head. But if the attitudes of the non-worshippers can keep us from worshipping we will never become worshippers, for they have always outnumbered us greatly.

Simon's criticism expressed an attitude of self-righteousness when he said, "If He knew what kind of person she was . . . ," inferring that Simon very well knew. The self-righteous always project that they know something that no one else knows, but the worshipper is only concerned with responding properly to the person he has come to know.

Throughout life, expressed attitudes involve responsive attitudes. Love extended generally induces a love response, while anger vented often stirs an angry retaliation. When this unnamed woman poured out her brokenness, humility, love, and sacrificial giving upon Jesus, He, in turn, released His attitudes toward her. The first such attitude was *forgiveness*. Jesus said, "Her sins, which are many, are forgiven; for she loved much . . ." (Luke 7:47). Simon had told Jesus that in his opinion the person who had been forgiven the most would love the most, but Jesus reversed it and said it is the love that produces the forgiveness. Salvation is more than a sinner forsaking his sins, it is a sinner responding to God's love!

The next three attitudes Jesus demonstrated to her are given by Luke in the last verse of this chapter, "And he said to the woman, Thy *faith* hath *saved* thee; go in *peace* (Luke 7:50, italics added). Faith, deliverance, and peace all have their origins in Christ Jesus. None of us can generate them, but all of us can receive them. They are reciprocal responses to our expressed attitudes of worship.

There is no greater place to receive faith than while worshipping at the feet of Jesus. Furthermore, no matter what we may need to be saved from (the Greek word Luke used is *sozo* which means "deliver, protect, heal, preserve, be whole, do well, save"), our complete salvation is vested in the Savior, and when we are worshipping Him our salvation is assured. Similarly, there is no peace like the peace a worshipper finds when he has completely poured out himself upon his Lord.

Attitudes are vitally important in all of us, for they color and control our actions. True worship will flow out of proper attitudes, but what is our attitude about the object of our worship? Just who is to receive worship? Is it but a name, or a person? Does our attitude towards who He is affect the way we respond to Him?

CHAPTER 10

THE OBJECT OF WORSHIP

In my travels throughout the world, I have watched persons of many different cultures bow until their foreheads almost touched the ground; kneel, or fully prostrate themselves for long periods before their god, while others crossed a cobblestone courtyard crawling on their hands and knees to do obeisance to their god. I've seen baskets of fruit presented to an idol, and have watched while sacrifices have been burned on a flaming altar. I've been a spectator as the worshippers marched in great ceremony, parading their idols through the streets of the city, singing, dancing and playing instruments in honor of their god. I've also observed obviously poor people drop coins into collection boxes or place money directly into the hands of their priest in return for some assistance in performing their worship. These sincere people sacrifice to pour out their adoration upon their gods, but it is all in vain, for they have chosen the wrong object of worship. In two separate psalms the futility of this worship is expressed in identical words:

The idols of the heathen are silver and gold, the work of men's hands. They have mouths, but they speak not; eyes have they, but they see not; they have ears, but they hear not; neither is there any breath in their mouths. They that

make them are like unto them: so is everyone
that trusteth in them.
(Psalm 115:4-8, 135:15-18).

How can worship offered to an inanimate object be
efficacious?

"To worship or not to worship" has never been the
question, for all of God's created beings are inherently
worshippers. No matter how vociferously he may deny it,
each person on earth is instinctively a worshipper. It is in
his genetic strain! The issue has never been, shall we
worship or not? It is more consistently a question of *who*
we will worship.

The object of our worship is always the greatest point
of controversy in worship. This controversy did not begin
with man here on earth. According to Isaiah 14, Lucifer's
fall was the result of high-level pride that caused him to
express a desire to become the object of Heaven's
worship. He has never lost this aspiration. From his
temptation of Eve in Eden to the temptation of Christ in
the wilderness, satan consistently recruited worshippers
from among earth's inhabitants, and he still does.

All fundamental Bible-believing Christians agree
with Jesus that God is the only acceptable object of
worship. They know of God's expressed hatred of idol
worship, and they have read in the Old Testament of
God's repeated punishment of those who worshipped
anything besides the true and living God. They accept,
intellectually at least, God's demand that He alone
should be worshipped.

Most of these same Christians have also memorized
Christ's pointed statement on worship from John 4:23.
"The hour cometh and now is when the true worshippers
shall worship the Father in spirit and in truth." And yet,

for all of their mental acquiescence to God's exclusive rights to their worship, even a casual observer will discover fundamental Christians offering worship to lesser gods in their lives.

If we will accept the dictionary's definition of worship as, "to adore, to revere, to exalt, to magnify, to dote, to admire or to esteem," then it becomes quite obvious that many Christians worship, to a lesser extent perhaps, many things that are beneath the image of God.

Some exalt their denomination in a manner that at least borders on worship. Others dote dangerously on their pastor, while still others magnify a doctrinal truth almost to the place of God Himself. Furthermore, we've all seen people, even God-fearing saints, so love possessions as to become worshippers of them, and others have disgusted us as they become worshippers of themselves.

Not that anyone intends for his affections to get so out of control as to direct his worship to something less than God, but still it happens all too frequently, for what we love soon becomes what we worship. Perhaps this is why the Bible so clearly commands us: "Love not the world, neither the things that are in the world. If any man love the world, the love of the Father is not in him" (1 John 2:15).

So the key to maintaining the divine monopoly in worship is to ". . . Love the Lord thy God with all thy heart, and with all thy soul, and with all thy mind, and with all thy strength . . ." (Mark 12:30). When everything within us loves God fully, He alone will be the object of our worship. Otherwise, we will be as vacillating in our worship as we are in our loving.

Unfortunately the propensity to idolatry is inherent in each of us. Worshipping something short of God seems more natural to us than worshipping God Himself, since we find it easier to relate to the tangible than to the intangible and to respond to the seen rather than to the unseen. Yet God is the only truly acceptable object of our worship.

Jesus told the woman of Samaria that the true worshippers would "worship the Father" (John 4:24), but few of us have a good concept of God the Father. At Mt. Sinai when God revealed Himself in fire, smoke, thunder, and lightning, and then spoke directly to Israel, the people were so terrified that they asked God to never do that again. So God sought to reveal Himself through the law as a God of law and order who was approachable through ordinances, means, and the mediacy of the priesthood, but the people found themselves unable to keep His laws and, furthermore, they preferred to let the priesthood become their substitute rather than their mediator in worship. If God revealed Himself in angelic form the people expected to drop dead, so at Bethlehem God revealed Himself as the God-man. He became a person like us in order to lead us to the person of God. As a baby He was non-threatening to all but Herod, and as a man he was understandable, lovable, and comfortable to men, women and children.

Jesus came not only to redeem us from sin but to reveal to us the Father. The Scripture says, "In many and various ways God spoke of old to our fathers by the prophets; but in these last days he has spoken to us by a Son, whom He appointed the heir of all things, through whom also He created the world. He reflects the glory of God and bears the very stamp of His nature, upholding the universe by His word of power" (Hebrews 2:1-3, RSV).

If you listen to Jesus speak you'll hear the voice of the Father, for Jesus said, "I have not spoken on my authority; the Father who sent me has himself given me commandments what to say and what to speak" (John 12:49 RSV). Look at Christ's marvelous works and see the Father at work, for Jesus also said, "The Son can do nothing by Himself. He does only what He sees the Father doing, and in the same way. For the Father loves the Son, and tells him everything He is doing" (John 5:19, 20 TLB). Everything about Jesus reveals the Father to us, and in becoming like us, Christ caused us to lose our fear of the Father. Through Christ, we've come to know, trust, and love the Father; therefore, we can worship Him.

Christ Jesus is not only a revelation of the Father to us, He is also our access to the Father. Everything in the Tabernacle in the wilderness is a type of Jesus. He is as much our means of approach unto the Father now as He was then. Paul declares this in saying, "For *through* Him we both have access *by* one Spirit *unto* the Father" (Ephesians 2:18, italics added).

Diagrammed, this verse would look like this:

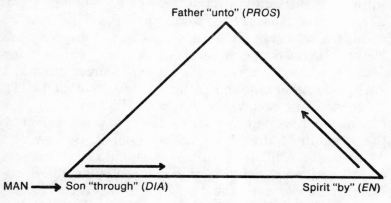

Jesus said virtually the same thing when He affirmed, "I am the way, the truth, and the life: no man cometh unto the Father, but by me" (John 14:6). At His ascension, Christ returned to heaven as our interceding

High Priest (see Hebrews 7:25), not to assure our salvation, for Calvary assured that, but to secure a permanent access to the Father so that we might be worshippers.

And so, dear brothers, now we may walk right into the very Holy of Holies where God is, because of the blood of Jesus. This is the fresh, new, life-giving way which Christ has opened up for us by tearing the curtain—His human body— to let us into the holy presence of God. And since this great High Priest of ours rules over God's household, let us go right in to God Himself, with true hearts fully sprinkled with Christ's blood to make us clean, and because we have been washed with the pure water." (Hebrews 10:19- 22, TLB)

Certainly "the hour . . . now is when the true worshippers shall worship the Father . . ." (John 4:23). Christ has both assured this and made it available to us.

But Christ is not only our access to worshiping the Father; He is a proper object of our worship Himself, for Jesus is in the Father. He taught us, "Believe me that I am in the Father, and the Father in me . . ." (John 14:11).

Christ Jesus receives worship in His own right, for men on earth worshipped Him. His birth was marked by the worship of the Magi, the shepherds, Simeon the prophet, and Anna the prophetess. During His ministry, Jesus received worship from a leper, a ruler, the Syro-Phoenician woman, the two Marys after the resurrection, His disciples, and many others. Surely Jesus would not have allowed men to worship Him if He was not worthy to receive it. In accepting worship Jesus Christ was admitting and declaring Himself to be very

God of very God; therefore, He is totally worthy of all worship.

Even the angels are instructed to worship Jesus (see Hebrews 1:6), and Matthew records the antiphonal chanting of worship by the angels at the birth of Jesus. In Heaven the Elders and the living creatures worship Jesus (see Revelation 4:9-11), and the Word declares that everyone shall worship Him (see Revelation 15:4 and Philippians 2:10-22).

Furthermore, most of our expressions of worship are either unto Jesus or in His name, for prayer is directed unto Him and in His name, and praise is generally concerned with Him and His works. Even our thanksgiving is directed to Him, as Paul did in saying, "... I thank Christ Jesus our Lord, who hath enabled me ..." (1 Timothy 1:12), and the rituals we observe are commemorative of Jesus.

However, whether we worship the Father through the Son or worship the Son in the Father, the level of our worship will be determined by our concept of the One we are worshipping and many of us are confused about Christ Jesus as was the woman at the well.

Jesus had revealed Himself to her as the Messiah, but she chose to see Him as a prophet (compare John 4:25, 29 with 19). The concept of the man at the well actually being the Messiah was too lofty for her; there had never been a Messiah, but there had been prophets and she could relate to that, so she, like we, lowered a divine revelation until it fit her past theology.

Every new move of God tends to be dragged down to the level of a prior move of God, and every fresh revelation God gives of Himself is apt to be diminished to a prior revelation with which we are already comfortably related. What it amounts to is that we never allow our concepts of God to enlarge. The majority of our singing, testifying, and talking about Jesus refers to Him as our Healer, Savior, Comforter, Blesser, Baptiser, Lover, and so forth. These are *roles* that He fills in His relationships with us, but they only illustrate a small facet of who He really is. To the sinner, Christ fills the role of a Savior; to the seeker, He becomes the Baptiser; to the sick, Jesus functions as the Healer; and to the sorrowful, Jesus becomes the Comforter. But the New Testament does not declare that He *is* any of these things. Consistently the New Testament declares that Jesus Christ *is Lord.*

Our initial introduction to Jesus was as one who met our needs, and many never allow Him to reveal anything else about Himself. But worship requires that we respond to someone higher than the Jesus of our discovery, or the Jesus who meets our needs. We need to worship the Christ of divine revelation; the Christ who is the Almighty God.

Perhaps this can best be understood by looking at the responses of John the Beloved Disciple. For over three years this young man lived and ministered with Jesus. It appears that he had a more intimate relation to Jesus than the other disciples, for he was with Jesus on the mount of transfiguration, in the garden, in the judgment hall, at the whipping post, and stood and watched the crucifixion. It was to this John that Jesus entrusted the care of his earthly mother. Yet we never once read of John worshipping Jesus during these days. It was not until many years later, when banished to the Isle of Patmos and receiving a vision of Jesus as the Ancient of Days, that John fell at His feet and worshipped Him (see Revelation 1). This, too, was the experience of Isaiah in the Old Testament. Until these great men began to see

Jesus as more than God's provided means for meeting men's needs they did not worship, but when they saw Him as God, worship was an inevitable response. Just as a substitute vision will produce a substitute response, a shallow concept will produce shallow worship.

Quite frequently over the years I have been with groups where God so honored the preaching of the Word that His presence sovereignly enveloped the congregation. When I have turned the service back to the leader, he has often responded by saying, "I don't know when I have ever sensed the presence of the Lord Jesus Christ like I do in this service tonight. Let's everyone bow his head . . . ."

What is said following that is pre-determined by that leader's concept of and orientation to Christ Jesus. If he is evangelistically inclined, he will say, ". . . I want all those who need to accept Jesus as Savior to come to the front right now." People come and get saved.

If he is a leader with a compassion for the sick his call will be, ". . . all who are suffering with pain, stand right where you are and we'll pray for you." They stand, and often they are healed.

While I believe in and practice altar calls upon occasion, I am often saddened that when the Lord actually makes His presence known we seek to work Him rather than worship Him. Knowing Him only as a meeter of our needs never inspires any higher worship than praise.

Much of the time that I travel my wife stays at home. When the tour is over, I look forward to having her meet me at the airport. I am so thankful to God that my delightful wife does not greet me at the airport with a quick hug and kiss and then begin immediately to tell me, "Honey, the furnace broke down, the roof is leaking, and we've got trouble with the car again. I'm so glad that my fix-it man is home again."

No, that's not how I am received back home after a period of absence. I'm welcomed, loved, fed, rested, and then she helps me find the list of things that need repairing. I am her fix-it man, and she knows that I will have everything fixed before I leave on my next tour. But she did not marry a repairman, she married a person; she relates to me for whom I am, not merely for what I can do for her. Until we see Christ Jesus as He is, not merely for the roles that He fills, we will never be able to worship Him.

Our challenge is to worship the Father, but God has revealed Himself as love, light and a consuming fire. We could not worship such concepts, so God became man, and they called His name Jesus. This Jesus is the express image of the Father, and comes both as a demonstration of the Father and as a revelation of Him. If we restrict our concept of Jesus to being the one who meets all of our human needs, we will also restrict our revelation of the Father, and, furthermore, we'll severely limit our worship responses.

It's this very confusion that makes it so imperative that a worshipper have the assistance of the Holy Spirit. The Spirit actually knows God the Father and God the Son, and as a member of that Godhead He dwells within the life of the believer. Worship without the aid of the Holy Spirit is probably impossible.

11

THE
HOLY SPIRIT
AND WORSHIP

I stood on the platform at a conference some years ago as the congregation released themselves to worship God in a way with which I was uncomfortable. I watched for a few moments and soon realized that they had come into a depth of sincerity and expression beyond my experience levels and I could not honestly reject it. Nonetheless, I could not participate in it from my inner being; I could only conform to their outer actions.

"I don't know how to worship!" I cried to the Lord.

"But I do," the Holy Spirit seemed to respond within me, "And I'll teach you, if you'll let me."

I must confess that I didn't learn to worship their way during that one service, for I found that learning is a progressive work of the Holy Spirit. Patient teacher that He is, He leads us progressively from where we are to where we should be in our worship. Throughout the months that followed, I would rise to a level of worship and find some invisible force hindering me from entering a higher level. I would see into the things of the Lord, and my heart would want to respond in adoration, but somehow I couldn't get the words out of my mouth; I just couldn't release my emotions. There was something between me and the God I deeply desired to respond to. Having already confessed any known sin in my life and not being aware of any wrong attitudes, I stood facing this invisible barrier completely stymied.

I was, and still am, convinced that anytime there is something between me and God in the time of worship, that that hindrance will never be on God's side, for there is absolutely nothing in God that prevents our worshipping Him. Nothing! That meant that the barrier was within me and I did not know what it was.

Sharing this with others has convinced me that my experience is not unique; they, too, have faced this invisible barrier to worship. Is not this the reason that God put His own Spirit within our hearts, to enable us to cry, "Abba, Father"? God knows what changes are necessary on man's side, rather than on His side, to make worshippers out of us, so by living within man's spirit, God is able to help us to overcome the barriers to worship that may be sin-generated, culturally-induced, or religiously engrained in us. Our training in life and religion have predetermined our responses to God, and our spirit has set up an automatic veto in our memory circuits so that the moment we seek to go beyond that ban our minds flash "does not compute" back to us. The Holy Spirit, working from within, begins to reprogram our conscious and subconscious minds to release us to worship God in fresh new ways.

It is to be expected, then, that Jesus would tell the woman at the well that the worshippers ". . . shall worship the Father in spirit and in truth. . . . God is a Spirit: and they that worship him must worship him in spirit and in truth" (John 4:23, 24). For while praise can be the product of the human spirit, worship is impossible without the aid of the Holy Spirit of God.

Oh yes, "Holy Spirit of God" is a correct title, for He is called this at least twenty-seven times in the Scriptures.

He is also called the "Spirit of the Lord" some thirty times, and the "Spirit of Christ" on repeated occasions. The Holy Spirit is an integral part of the Triune Godhead, for He is as united with the Father as is Jesus Christ. He is presented in the Bible as the promise of the Father and the gift of Christ and, in a way that is easier stated than explained, God's Spirit establishes residence in the lives of individual believers, for Paul says, "Know ye not that ye are the temple of God, and that the Spirit of God dwelleth in you?" (1 Corinthians 3:16). It is this indwelling Spirit of God that becomes the channel for God's graces and self-revelation to come to be effectual in the lives of Christians, ". . . because the love of God is shed abroad in our hearts by the Holy Ghost which is given unto us" (Romans 5:5).

In the *International Standard Bible Encyclopedia* Phillip Wendell Crannel is quoted as saying, "Worship . . . is the response of God's Spirit in us to that Spirit in Him, whereby we answer, 'Abba, Father,' deep calling unto deep" (page 3112). Worship of the Father, then, is not merely man's spirit on earth responding to God's Spirit in Heaven; rather it is God's Spirit in man responding to God's Spirit in God. It is the Holy Spirit worshipping through us, and how much more capable He is at this than we are.

True worship has always been both spiritual and in the Spirit, so when we worship God through Jesus Christ in the power of the Holy Spirit our worship will be both "in Spirit and in truth."

New Testament worship has two essentials in it that are lacking in the Old Testament. First, it is Christological in its orientation. Whereas the Old Testament worshipper approached God through the rituals and sacrifices of the temple, the New Testament worshipper stands in a personal relation of sonship to God on the basis of adoption in Christ Jesus. He is more than a suppliant; he is a son. He approaches God not through the services of an earthly mediator, but through the mediation of Christ Himself. Today's believer need not approach God through means of structure only, he has the resident Spirit of God to channel his worship directly into the Holy of Holies.

God, come in flesh to fulfill His work of grace in men, has given worship a depth and a content which was totally lacking in the Old Testament. Surely, then, our worship should not be less enthusiastic, joyful, or expressive than theirs, should it?

The second essential to be found in New Testament worship that was not obvious in the worship of the Old Testament saints is that the ministry of the Holy Spirit is now available to all believers, whereas it seemed to be restricted to selected leaders in the Old Testament. This is evidenced in the early work of the Spirit in an individual's life as the Spirit guides him into a conversion experience. Before conversion we were spiritually dead, and the Psalmist declares that, "The dead praise not the Lord" (Psalm 115:17). Prior to conversion we were "children of darkness," so terrified by the light of God's countenance that we dared not come into His presence. But since our conversion we are "light in the Lord." This converting work of the Spirit, whereby former children of the devil become children of God who are partakers of the divine nature, makes it easy for us to worship God in praise, song, prayer, and in ordinances.

A further work of the Holy Spirit that is available to the New Testament believer is the infilling of the Spirit, or, as some prefer to call it, the baptism of the Spirit. It is the experience that the disciples received on the day of

Pentecost, and to which Paul alluded when he inquired of the saints in Ephesus, "Have ye received the Holy Ghost since ye believed' " (Acts 19:2). When they replied that they had not so much as heard about the Holy Spirit, Paul laid his hands upon them, and ". . . the Holy Ghost came on them; and they spake with tongues, and prophesied" (Acts 19:6). Later when Paul wrote a letter to this church he admonished them, "And be not drunk with wine, wherein is excess; but be filled with the Spirit; speaking to yourselves in psalms and hymns and spiritual songs, singing and making melody in your heart to the Lord" (Ephesians 5:18, 19), thereby linking this infilling of the Spirit to worshipping God.

But this indwelling Spirit of God not only gives us a melodious worship response to God, He also bears the *fruit* of the spirit within our lives. This effectively replaces much of our carnal nature with God's divine nature, for after listing the horrendous works of the flesh, Paul writes, "But the fruit of the Spirit is love, joy, peace, longsuffering, gentleness, goodness, faith, meekness, temperance . . ." (Galatians 5:22, 23). As a corrective instruction Paul challenged the Christians in Galatia to "walk in the Spirit, and ye shall not fulfill the lust of the flesh" (Galatians 5:16). Since the greatest hindrances to worship are inherent in our natural lives, this work of the indwelling Spirit in freeing us from the works of the flesh breaks the bondages that prohibit, or greatly restrict, our worship by the very fruit of His presence, for our unloving nature is replaced with His fruit of love, and our inner turmoil is superseded by His peace, while His gentleness overrides our harshness. When we are able to worship God with the character of the Holy Spirit, our worship is accepted.

Furthermore, this indwelling Spirit helps the believer

in his worship through the operation of the *gifts* of the Spirit, as we saw in Chapter 2.

These spiritual energies that enable us to know things about which we could have no knowledge apart from the Spirit's impartation make worship a knowing experience as well as an emotional experience. The word of wisdom, word of knowledge, and discerning of spirits, as they are listed in 1 Corinthians 12:8-10, is God sharing what He knows with His unknowing saints, and this knowing aids, abets, and accommodates our worship.

The three spiritual gifts that enable us to perform wonders in the spiritual, faith, gifts of healing, and the working of miracles (see 1 Corinthians 12:9, 10) bridge the gap between earth and heaven by demonstrating the availability of spiritual might and authority in our time. These are, of course, powerful evangelistic tools, but they also inspire worship in the lives of Christian believers as well.

Probably the most prevalent of these gifts during times of worship are the vocal gifts which Paul lists as "prophecy, divers kinds of tongues, and interpretation of tongues" (see 1 Corinthians 12:10). In the fourteenth chapter of 1 Corinthians, where Paul gives some instruction in the proper use of these giftings in the public assembly, he says that the tongues are a communication from man's spirit to God, and where this is interpreted we can all join the speaker in glorifying God, while the expression of prophecy is God's communication to man through man. All are concerned with spiritually enabling us to participate freely in the two-way communication that characterizes true worship. It is communication of our spirit that is aided by the Holy Spirit.

The use of the tongue in worship is explained by Paul when he says, "... he that speaketh in an unknown tongue speaketh not unto men, but unto God: for no man understandeth him; howbeit in the spirit he speaketh mysteries" (1 Corinthians 14:2). I would understand this to suggest that by using a language unknown to the speaker, the Holy Spirit is able to by-pass the censorship of the conscious mind and to worship God at a much higher level than would otherwise be possible, for all of our communication with God is regulated by our concepts of God plus our faith levels. This often limits our worship drastically, but when the Holy Spirit can worship through us according to His concepts, and at His faith level, our worship indeed "speaketh mysteries." When a believer submits to the work of the Spirit in sharing God's character through the *fruit*, and in sharing the charismata of God through the operation of the gifts of the Spirit, he is already a long way toward being a true worshipper.

But this is not the only way the New Testament believer has the advantage of the Holy Spirit to help in worshipping. All of the elements of worship that we discussed in Chapter 8 are greatly assisted by the Holy Spirit. For instance, prayer, so essential to worship, comes with the assistance of the Spirit. Paul, who was known for his prayer ministry, declared, "I will pray with my spirit—by the Holy Spirit that is within me; but I will also pray intelligently—with my mind and understanding" (1 Corinthians 14:15, Amplified). Prayer without the help of the Spirit can be a laborious and unfruitful task.

Praise, which is often the vocal end of worship is, fundamentally, a rejoicing of the Spirit as Paul declared to the church in Philippi, "For we (Christians) are the true circumcision, who worship God in spirit and by the Spirit of God, and exult and glory and pride ourselves in

Jesus Christ . . ." (Philippians 3:3, Amplified).

Furthermore, the confession of sins and confession of faith is both a conviction of and a confession by the Holy Spirit, for Paul declared, "No one can (really) say Jesus is (my) Lord, except by and under the power and influence of the Holy Spirit" (1 Corinthians 12:3. TAB).

Even the reading of the Scripture as worship must be illuminated by the Spirit, and preaching, which God has chosen to be a part of worship, must be in the power and the demonstration of the Spirit; otherwise it is not part of, nor will it produce, worship.

Worship is not a performable act without the help of the Spirit, whether we choose to worship through means of the sacraments or a more free form of expression to God. We don't know how to worship, so we must be guided in each worship experience. The way we worshipped yesterday may not be the way the Spirit would lead to worship today, and the only way we will really know the route into God's presence for the present moment is to maintain a sweet communion with the Holy Spirit so that He can lead us into the Holy Place of communion with God.

When I was in South Africa I was given a copy of *New Vision*, a magazine which is published by Vision Publications as a part of the ministry of the Christian Interdenominational Fellowship of South Africa. In this Volume 3, #6 issue they had an interview with the Rev. Brian Bird of St. Nicholas, an Anglican Parish in Port Elizabeth. In answer to the question "You mentioned the Holy Spirit giving life to the Body?" the Rev. Bird answered:

Yes! The Holy Spirit prevents our worship from becoming stereotyped and dull. The glorious thing is that the Spirit blows where He wills and

He is always fresh, never dull or routine. In a sense, we have to 'open the windows' at the beginning of a service and ask Him to blow upon us and lead us. It is obviously risky if we don't like draughts and sometimes we keep the windows tightly closed! If we fall into the trap of saying: "This is how it worked last week, let's try and do the same thing today," we will be 'making it work' and we will lose the freshness, the life of the Spirit. Therefore we use the elements of the liturgy without following it precisely if the Spirit leads us elsewhere. There is a responsibility to be open to the Spirit and aware of where He is taking us. The Holy Spirit wants to glorify Jesus and we most certainly do; so the result must be worship, and that worship will be different each time.

To become worshippers "in spirit and in truth" we must learn to follow the gentle nudgings of the Spirit; to move with the Spirit. He is a person, you know, and He has varying moods. Whatever mood He may indicate we would do well to stop everything else and follow it. If He is present in a rejoicing disposition, we should give ourselves to enthusiastic rejoicing. If the Spirit seems to be in a giving mood, we would wisely give an offering to God. Whatever He is doing, we must do it with Him, for that will bring us into genuine worship.

Worship is always a *now* act. But doesn't this present problems when we are separated from the sacraments and the church structure? Where is the proper place of worship for the Spirit-inspired believer?

CHAPTER

12

THE PLACE OF WORSHIP

For the second time in ten years, and for a full eighteen months, the army of Nebuchadnezzar, King of Babylon, maintained a tight siege around the city of Jerusalem. Zedekiah, uncle to Nebuchadnezzar, had been appointed as a caretaker king after the first fall of Jerusalem. But he rebelled against the king of Babylon and now he found his kingdom under a second siege. With starvation taking its toll inside the city, Zedekiah tried to sneak away in the middle of the night but he was captured. Then he was forced to watch while his sons were slain, after which his captors put out his eyes, bound him with fetters of brass, and carried him to Babylon.

At the first capture of Jerusalem, the Babylonian army had stripped the house of the Lord of all its treasures. This time they completely destroyed both the temple and the city of Jerusalem, and marched the surviving residents to Babylon to become slaves, leaving only the poor of the land to "be vinedressers and husbandmen" (see 2 Kings 25).

The people who remained in the land of necessity intermarried with the populace in the surrounding areas and formed the group that was later identified as the Samaritans. Having neither city or temple, these Samaritans were forced to worship on the mountain, patterning their religion after the Jewish tradition but without the benefit of the Levitical priesthood. Because they did not suffer the rigors of the captivity and since they did not keep their Jewish lines pure, when the dispersed Jews returned to rebuild the city and temple under Ezra and Nehemiah, these Samaritans were despised by the repatriated Jews. They refused to have any dealings with them, thus forcing the Samaritans to continue in the form of religion they had developed during their caretaking years: their worshipping on the mountain.

This formed the basis of the argument of the woman at the well when Jesus spoke to her about worship. "Our fathers worshipped in this mountain; and ye say, that in Jerusalem is the place where men ought to worship," the woman told Jesus. "Jesus saith unto her, Woman, believe me, the hour cometh when ye shall neither in the mountain, nor yet at Jerusalem, worship the Father" (see John 4:20, 21).

To this woman the issue of worship was all tied up in your way or our way; your place or our place; your rituals or our rituals; your heritage or our heritage; on the mountain or in the city? She is not, however, to be condemned, for we have the same questions when the matter of worship is discussed, only we phrase them differently. We want to know whether worship is best performed with sacraments and ritual, or in a more free-form style. Some are convinced that we cannot worship in organized religion, using liturgical forms and practices, feeling that this is spiritual Babylon, so they associate exclusively with para-church groups.

Most Protestants are convinced that none can worship in a Catholic setting, while many Catholics have asked me if Protestants ever worship, for they have only seen them work at their religion. Still others get greatly disturbed over whether the worship is in the soul or spirit; the emotions or the will.

While there may be something to be said in each of these arguments, Jesus chose to bypass these fundamental hedges to worship and go to the real core of the issue. "But the hour cometh," He said, "and now is, when the true worshippers shall worship the Father in spirit and in truth" (John 4:23). Ignoring the mountain/city based argument, Jesus stated quite simply that true worship occurs in the spirit. The Greek word He used is *pneuma* which is translatable as "breath" or "spirit," and is used for God's Spirit, man's spirit, and demon spirits. Whether this refers to worship in the Holy Spirit, which would be theologically accurate, or to worship in the human spirit, which is equally correct, may depend upon our understanding of the context. In the King James Version the translators consistently use a capital "S" when they feel that the context indicates that it is the Holy Spirit, and here they have used the lower case. I checked over thirty other translations of the New Testament and found only two of them who disagreed with the King James, and these are not translations now in popular use. The context here would seem to indicate that Jesus is referring to the human spirit and simply saying that worship does not take place in shrines or cities, but in the spirit of the worshipper.

This in no way violates the teaching of Ephesians 2:18 which we have already discovered tells us that we worship by means of the Holy Spirit. The Spirit of God, is, indeed, the *means* of worship, but man's spirit is the *place* where worship occurs.

Man was created a tripartite being, for he was made in the image of the Triune God Who is Father, Son and Holy

Spirit (see Genesis 1:26). In his tripartite being, man is *spirit* with an active will and an implanted God-consciousness; man is *soul* with an intellect and emotions; and man is *body* with its self-consciousness and world-consciousness. In God's specific creation man's spirit dominated and directed man, but sin inverted this creation, giving fundamental control of the life to man's body. It takes the regenerative work of Christ in God to restore man to God's original plan wherein he can be directed from his spirit. Diagrammed in pyramid format the contrast would appear as:

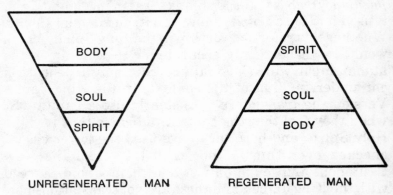

Because what is uppermost in a person's life controls the rest of his life it is obvious that the unregenerate must respond Godward ("worship") from their physical nature. It is interesting that most people who come to God for salvation come because of an extreme personal need in their physical life. As has been wisely stated, "Few persons come to God because they want Him; they come to Him because they need Him."

While the unconverted must respond Godward from their physical nature the Christian may do so, too, and far too many Christians attempt to worship in the physical area of their lives without ever learning how to worship God in their inner, eternal, spirit.

It should be obvious that religious ritual can be performed in any of the three areas of a person's life, for man ultimately responds Godward with all that he is: spirit, soul, and body. Bodily reverence or respect toward God can be seen in lifting of the hands, standing, prostrating before the Lord, bowing, clapping the hands, waving the hands, kneeling, dancing, singing, and so forth. These may be done as an expression of worship in response to the direction of man's spirit or they may be done as a religious exercise that never gets close to true worship.

Furthermore, there are people who involve their bodies in masochistic actions as acts of worship by maiming the body, wounding themselves, by undue fastings, or denying their bodies needed sleep or proper recreation. They feel the more miserable their body feels and looks the greater the level of their worship. It is sad that they cannot realize that their actions are marring a creation that was made in the image of God.

Still others, whose approach to God is primarily physical, depend upon special robes, special make-up or religious jewelry (which I call holy hardware) and consider that the wearing of them constitutes worship.

But for every person who attempts to worship God through purely physical actions, there must be a thousand who reach after God in soul devotion, for singing, shouting, praising, weeping, and emotional expressions may be channels of worship in the spirit, *or* they may be done as a substitute for worship.

Soulish worship is *feeling* motivated and depends upon external impetus rather than divine anointing. It can so duplicate true spiritual "feelings" as to pass for true worship, since we are limited to one set of emotions which are played upon by both our soul and our spirit. If a "worship service" requires emotional stories and psychological impetus to stir it into being, it is very likely soulish worship. So much of America's "evangelistic services" and "gospel music" are soulish both in origin and in result. That men's emotions are deeply touched is undeniable, but unless their spirits contact God there will be neither conversion or worship, for both are an action of the Spirit of God upon the spirit of man, and soul is not spirit any more than body is spirit.

While fully knowing that religious ritual, which men called worship, was being performed in the physical and soulish realms, Jesus told the woman at the well that ". . . true worshippers shall worship the Father in spirit . . ." (John 4:23). In saying this Jesus not only disassociated worship from physical and soulish actions performed in a specific place, but He said that worship would occur in the spirit of the worshipper. Actions of the body and soul may form a prelude to worship, or may become expressions of the worship, but the true worship takes place when a person's spirit contacts God's Spirit.

Throughout the Old Testament this place of contact was often associated with a physical location. Jacob had his Bethel, Moses had his Sinai, and the children of Israel had their tabernacle. But in each of these the key was not the location or the methodology employed to express their worship. The characteristic factor of worship in each place was that these men met God. That is still the hub of all worship experiences, and to meet God, man must come to God.

Probably the greatest cause of failure in worship is our attempt to perform it before we arrive in God's presence. It was because Jacob met God at Bethel on at least two occasions that he could worship, and it was because every time Moses climbed to the top of Sinai he found the presence of God that he was able to worship. Later, it was when the High Priest entered the Holy of Holies and shared in the Skekinah of God that he could worship beyond the mere performance of ritualistic acts. And so it will be with us.

But where is God in the New Testament economy? We are taught that, "Whosoever shall confess that Jesus is the Son of God, God dwelleth in him, and he in God," and "Hereby know we that we dwell in him, and He in us because he hath given us of His Spirit" (1 John 4:15, 13). God dwells in men. But where in men has God taken up residence? Paul declared that "The Spirit itself beareth witness with our spirit that we are the children of God" (Romans 8:16). God's Spirit resides in man's spirit, not in his body or soul; hence it is imperative that worship be performed in man's spirit, for that is his contact point with God's Spirit.

But this concept is not to negate the teaching of the entire Bible that ". . . God is in heaven, and thou upon earth . . ." (Ecclesiastes 5:2), and, ". . . our God is in the heavens: he hath done whatsoever he hath pleased" (Psalm 115:3). Because Christians worship where God is, they must have access and rights to heaven, which answers to the Holy of Holies of the tabernacle and the temple. Since at the death of Jesus at Calvary the thick veil in Herod's temple was torn from the top to the bottom indicating that the perfect sacrifice of God's Son had met all of God's holy claims, therefore, access into His presence could be extended to all in whom His Spirit had taken residence. The writer to the Hebrews expressed it this way: "Having therefore, brethren, boldness to enter into the holiest by the blood of Jesus, by a new and living way, which he has consecrated for us, through the veil, that is to say, his flesh; and having an high priest over the house of God; let us draw near with a true heart in full assurance of faith . . ." (Hebrews 10:19-22). Access to God in His heaven has been assured both to the individual believer and to the collective body of believers that form the Church. The priesthood of all believers is consistently taught throughout the Bible, and when believer-priests meet together in the name of the Lord Jesus Christ they, as a company of priests, can lay hold, by faith, upon God's promised right of entrance, and they may enter the Holy Place to worship Almighty God in the beauty of holiness. Hence heaven cannot be too far away, for a group of saints can step from the church pews into the divine presence in but a moment of time. It is not so much a matter of heaven coming down, as with Jacob, as it is the reality of the believer-priests going up into the spiritual heavens where their great High Priest awaits to assist them in their worship of God.

Worship, then, is far more than the awe that beautiful architecture can produce, or the reverence that vestments may incite, or the sense of sacredness the sacraments can bring, or even the stirred emotions that music often produces; worship is the interaction of man's spirit with God in a loving response. It begins in the spirit of man and, with the aid of the Spirit of God, ascends into the very presence of God Himself in the Heaven of heavens.

This is why the issue of *where* we should worship can never be germane. True worship is not dependent on buildings or any external stimuli, for God is worshipped in man's heart and in God's Heaven. This can occur when that person is in the world's most beautiful cathedral or when he is milking the cows in a barn. Worship can take place with the aid of beautiful music or when surrounded by the insistent noise of everyday commerce. It requires neither privacy nor the public performance of God's appointed leaders in the church. A thousand things may assist a believer in his worship of God, but fundamentally that worship is an inner reaching out and up to God, so where it takes place on the face of this earth is totally irrelevant, for it must reach God in Heaven before it can become a full worship experience anyway, and that is where true worshippers worship.

In saying that the true worshippers will worship in the spirit, was Jesus merely separating the true from the false worshippers, or did He have something further in mind? Could He also have been referring to the use of truth in worship instead of deceit?

13

THE
TRUTH
IN WORSHIP

In stating to the woman at the well that "the true worshippers shall worship the Father in spirit and in truth" (John 4:23), Jesus established at least three premises: first, that there can be true worshippers; second, that there is such a thing as true worship; and third, that there must be truth in worship.

Throughout the book we have been looking at true worshippers. Among the factors that separate true from false worshippers is their relationship to God, their motivation for worship, and their expression of that worship. The Greek word that Jesus used for "worshippers" is *proskunetes* which is the noun form of the verb *proskenien* that is translated as "worship" throughout John 4. But the noun form appears only here in the Bible. It indicates that a true worshipper is one who has such a love relationship with God that he has become a lover; he can "kiss towards," which is what the verb form means.

True worship must flow from a genuine relationship with God. A good relationship with a church may produce a good worker, but only a warm relationship with God can produce a true worshipper. As someone has said, "Worship is the upspring of a heart that has known the Father as a Giver, the Son as Savior, and the Holy

Spirit as the Indwelling Guest." To this I would add that this knowing must be experiential and current. Warm spirits produce worshipping hearts!

Not only must a true worshipper have a vital relationship with God, he must also have correct motivations in his worship. His goal must be to give unto the Lord rather than to get from Him. Worship which attempts to "soften up" God so as to induce Him to do for us is improperly motivated and cannot be called true worship. The purest motivation for worship is love that bubbles out of the spirit of man like a spring of living water.

Furthermore, true worshippers will manifest accurate expressions of their worshipful feelings. Their love will be poured out in an unrestrained manner when they are in the presence of Christ. They will not allow themselves to be limited by the traditions of men, or bound by the worship ritual of their religious heritage. Neither will they embrace extra-biblical expressions, for they will choose to be Bible-directed in all of their responses.

In speaking of true worship, Jesus may well have been referring to the tremendous contrast between worshipping the true and living God and worshipping idols. While few Americans bow before carved images to worship them as gods, we are a nation of idol worshippers as certainly as any heathen country. It's just that our idols are more sophisticated than carved logs or molten metal. Some of religion's most beautiful rituals fall short of true worship, for they are not offered unto God but unto man. Others who worship are deeply involved in self-worship, and self is a very subtle idol, for it possesses that ability to intrude itself into our holiest moments. Paul warned us that, ". . . in the last days perilous times shall come. For men shall be lovers of their own selves . . . lovers of pleasures more than lovers of God" (2 Timothy 3: 1, 2, 4).

Love of self and self-indulgence go hand in hand, and the worship of material possessions is almost an obsession with many, for Americans have had a longstanding love affair with *things.* Our culture teaches us to love things and to use people to get them, while God teaches us to love people and to use things to bless them. Too frequently, cars, homes, boats, guns, and wardrobes are cherished, treasured, and idolized with emotions that should be poured out in worshipping God. The Psalmist told us, ". . . if riches increase, set not your heart upon them" (Psalm 62:10). We dare not Christianize the American dream and teach prosperity as indication of God's approval of our lives, lest we find ourselves worshipping what the world has unsuccessfully worshipped for generations.

Nothing could take us farther from true worship than demon worship. Behind most idols is a demonic power that accepts all of the worship ascribed to idols, whether they are stone or the sophisticated varieties. America's obsession with the occult is nothing more or less than demon worship; some people now openly worship satan himself. Even in our Christian churches some persons place such an undue emphasis on our authority over demons that it borders on demon worship. Some Christians talk more with demons than with God, while others know more demon names than divine names. Some believers have read more books on demons than on God, while still other Christians live in terrorizing fear of demons; fear is to the demonic what faith is to the divine. When we are controlled by our fears we become worshippers of the demonic in the sense that we submit to their fear-inspired commands rather than to God's divinely inspired Word.

The list of things short of God that are worshipped by

people today would be nearly endless. Some so worship money that they have become "i-dollar-ters" while others worship business, pleasure, power and family.

Whether our veneration is for science, angels, nature, or service it obviously is not true worship, for it does not have the true God as its object. All worship not directed to the true God is *ipso facto idolatry.*

Besides all of this, Jesus said that a true worshipper would worship "in spirit and in *truth*" (John 4:23, italics added). Communion with God must be on His level. Since He is truth by nature, the one prerequisite for entry into God's realized presence is a true heart. "Let us all come forward and draw near with true (honest and sincere) hearts in unqualified assurance and absolute conviction engendered by faith" (Hebrews 10:22, TAB).

Not only must a worshipper be truthful in his approach and communion with God, but worshipping will reveal the truth to the worshipper. It will unfold to us truth about God, because we learn more about a person by being with him for one day than by reading about him for several months. Then we will learn the truth about ourselves as we see ourselves as God sees us.

In Matthew 15:21-28 we are told about a resident of Canaan, whom Mark calls a Syrophoenician, who seems to have heard that Jesus was going to visit the area of Tyre and Sidon. She practically met the boat at the shore, and the moment she saw Jesus she cried, "Have mercy on me, O Lord, thou son of David; my daughter is grievously vexed with a devil" (Matthew 15:22). She may have heard that blind Bartemeus was healed by yelling a similar cry or that two pairs of blind men, on widely separate occasions, had been restored to sight by crying this plea, for somehow this formula seemed to crop up repeatedly in the stories that had come out of Jerusalem. It had always seemed to work. Until now, that is. For no matter how earnestly, loudly, or passionately she cried this formula, Jesus "answered her not a word" (Matthew 15:23).

The actions of the disciples proved that she had been heard, for they pled with Jesus to send her away to get rid of the disturbance. But instead of complying with their request, Jesus replied: "I am not sent but unto the lost sheep of the house of Israel" (Matthew 15:24). In this one stage whisper, spoken loudly enough for the woman to plainly hear, Jesus unmasked the deceit and hypocrisy of her petitioning. She had been claiming a non-existent relationship with Christ, for in imploring Him as the "Son of David" she was apparently claiming to be an Israelite, a daughter of David. This was untrue, since the Gospel writers clearly identify her as a Gentile. But because she did not feel that Gentiles had any claim upon Christ, she masqueraded as a daughter of Israel who had covenant claims on the "Son of David." All this pretense got for her was total silence.

When God gives us the silent treatment, it is usually because we, too, are claiming a non-existent relationship. We, like her, pick up formulae that have worked beautifully for others and cry them religiously, whether they work or not. But unless we have the relationship that goes with the formula it will not work.

How many who have never been born again pray, "Our Father which art in Heaven"? Carnal Christians use the prayer language of the true bride, while the rebellious plead with God in their hour of trouble with the same expressions as the submitted saints. This will always be met by divine silence. God does not respond to hypocrisy, since He is truth by nature, hence we are instructed to ". . . draw near with a *true* heart . . ." (Hebrews 10:22, italics added). Any form of deceit will deny us an audience with God. Someone has said, "Either live it or don't lip it."

Nevertheless, we go on giving lip service to the words that meant life to our fathers and to the founders of our denominations, often unaware that we have only the liturgy, not the life, of these men. We have expressed the words as fact for so long that we are unaware that they have become a fable, or we have claimed a non-existent faith for so long that we cannot recognize our fraud. What can bring us out of our guile back into His grace? Worship in spirit and in truth!

Immediately after Jesus unmasked this imposter, she came "and worshipped him, saying, Lord, help me" (Matthew 15:25). Very likely, she prostrated herself before Him, perhaps even grabbing Him by the ankles and kissing His feet. She completely submitted herself to Him and poured out both her worship and her plea for help. And it worked. It always works! Worship is a door-opener that gives the supplicant access to God. If we can claim no covenant that will afford us entrance to Christ, we can open the door to His presence with worship. When our faith has failed and we falter in our approach to God, we can always fall back on worship, for worship is a consistent door-opener, to both the converted and unconverted alike, for all men have been invited to worship God. God declares, "shall all flesh come to worship before me, saith the Lord" (Isaiah 66:23). John saw a great company in Heaven singing the song of Moses and the song of the Lamb, ending it with these words: ". . . all nations shall come and worship before thee" (Revelation 15:4). Worship will open the door to God for anyone.

It is only fair to point out, however, that this door-opener to Christ automatically becomes an open door, allowing Him to get to us. Immediately after this daughter of Canaan began to worship Jesus, He began to probe into the depths of her heart. "It is not meet to take the children's bread," He said, "and to cast it to dogs" (Matthew 15:26). "You've claimed to be a daughter of Abraham, but in the eyes of Abraham's children you're nothing but a dog." These have always seemed like harsh words, but they were spoken by the world's most perfect gentleman. Christ was not condemning her, He was merely unveiling her to herself. He was causing her to not think more highly of herself than she ought to think (see Romans 12:3). J.B. Phillips translates this verse:

Don't cherish exaggerated ideas of yourself or your importance, but try to have a sane estimate of your capabilities by the light of the faith that God has given to you all.

Our Lord was merely helping to adjust this woman's self-concept, and He did it while she was worshipping. As she was exalting Him in worship, He was exposing her worthlessness. While she spoke of His Majesty ("Lord"), He spoke of her hypocrisy. His goal was not to depreciate her, but to help her appreciate her true relationship to Himself; until she did, He could not respond to her without condoning her falsehood. But if she would accept His appraisal and respond accordingly, He could and would minister to her need. Truth can relate to truth.

Isn't it when we are worshipping that God reveals us to ourselves? It was so with Isaiah, for he, who was likely the most godly man of his generation, when caught up into God's presence cried out:

Woe is me! for I am undone; because I am a man of unclean lips, and I dwell in the midst of a people of unclean lips: for mine eyes have seen the King, the Lord of hosts. (Isaiah 6:5)

Isaiah did not have this awareness when in the courts of earthly kings to whom he is reputed to have been a tutor, but when worship brought him into the presence of the heavenly King, he not only saw the Lord sitting upon a throne, "high and lifted up" (Isaiah 6:1), but he saw himself defiled and dirty. It is only when we are in the presence of heaven's Majestic King that we gain a true picture of ourselves. Compared with another, we may look great, but contrasted to Him, our artificial glory is revealed for what it really is.

So the Lord's response to the woman's worship was to call her a dog. How did she handle that? She said: "Truth, Lord" (Matthew 15:27). For until we acquiesce to His appraisal, communication with Him is ended. He has revealed our position and our condition; the next move is ours.

Admitting the truth that she was as separated from a covenant relationship with Christ as a dog is beneath his owner did not devastate this woman. She wisely changed her style of approach to match His estimate of her and gained everything she desired. She merely said, "yet the dogs eat of the crumbs which fall from their master's table" (Matthew 15:27). "If I am a dog, don't deny me a dog's privileges!" No greater principle can be learned than to approach Christ consistent with our true natures. If we're "a dog" and our natures have not been changed by a divine transformation, we can sit up, wag our tail, and lick the hand of the Master. If we're an infant in Christ, we can make pleasant "gooing" sounds and smile a lot. If we're a toddler, we can crawl to Him, pat Him, and say "da-da." But for a mature saint to do this would be ridiculous. Mature saints should approach Christ as a Christian adult.

We need not await a voice from heaven saying, "This is my beloved Son, in whom I am well pleased . . ." (Matthew 17:5) before coming to God. We can come just as we are. He can cleanse us as surely as He cleansed Isaiah, and change us as completely as He changed Nebuchadnezzar or Saul of Tarsus. We merely need to respond to Him as we are and from where we are, and it is worship that opens the door for this revelation to come to us.

It is, indeed, worship that brings us into a right relationship with God and with ourselves, and this revealed truth about ourselves can help us to stop staring at what we were and to start seeing what we are becoming in Christ Jesus. This will enable us to trade condemnation for cleansing and introspection for acceptance. We can see ourselves as Sons of God, heirs of God, and joint heirs with Christ Jesus.

Truth is costly. "Buy the truth, and sell it not" (Proverbs 23:23) is wise admonition. The truth about ourselves can be especially costly, but worship that costs us nothing obviously has little or no value to us. What is a proper price tag to be put on worship?

CHAPTER

14

THE PRICE OF WORSHIP

In the Tabernacle in the wilderness, which is a pattern of things in heaven, worship was demonstrated in type at the Golden Altar of incense which was positioned in front of the veil that separated the Holy of Holies from the Holy Place, and midway betwen the Golden Candlestick and the Table of Shewbread. God had commanded that every time a priest came into the Holy Place he was to take a handful of the specially compounded incense and sprinkle it upon the living coals that perpetually glowed upon this altar. The resulting cloud of perfumed smoke filtered through the thin linen veil that separated God from the priests. It filled the priestly compartment with its fragrance and saturated the clothing, hair, and skin of the priest, himself thereby making the fragrance of God's presence available to the common man in the outer court.

This was a visual demonstration of worship that teaches the New Testament believer-priest to offer the worship of prayer, thanksgiving, worship, and adoration when he comes into the presence of the Lord so that the worshipper's spirit, soul, and body will be permeated with the fragrance of God. It only takes a handful of worship incense to create a cloud of God's presence. But God wants that handful to be offered every time we go into the soul-spirit compartment of our lives.

For the priest to burn incense every time he went into the Holy Place, whether he entered to replace oil in the lamps, to trim the wicks of those lamps, to set the table of shewbread, or for whatever reason, was obviously a costly procedure, since we would suppose that there were many daily trips into this priestly compartment.

Furthermore, the incense itself was costly. It was composed of four ingredients that were blended in equal proportions, and none of these were commonly available to the Israelites. Stacte, onycha, galbanum, and frankincense had to be gathered from their respective sources and brought to the priests who then broke it into small pieces, beat it into powder, and blended it evenly so that it could be burned before the Lord. Whatever application one might choose to make of these four principal ingredients we must admit that our worship must come to a central place, be broken, beaten (contrited), and blended in order to be available for burning. This is costly in time, effort, emotion, and devotion, but worship always carries a price tag.

A further price that was attached to this incense was that it could be used for no other purpose than the worship of God. Any person caught using this same fragrance was to be stoned to death by the priests. There could be no "mass production" to bring the price down. God is very jealous of our worship and declares, ". . . Thou shalt worship the Lord thy God, and him only shalt thou serve" (Matthew 4:10). Emotional enthusiasm, although easier to generate, cannot substitute for worship, nor can worship be used for anything or anyone but God. It is our "tree in the garden," the fruit of which belongs exclusively to God. We, like Adam, may not eat the fruit of it.

While I was writing this chapter I was the guest

speaker at a breakfast gathering of Christians. The worship leader started by singing a chorus about the devil and, of course, our authority over him. The second chorus was directed to the devil himself, and the third chorus projected that we were an army that had the devil on the run. Only after that were we directed to sing about Jesus. The worship time was wasted and fell completely flat, for not only had we given satan top billing by calling attention to him first, but we had mixed our worship in offering some to the demonic (for all public attention given to them is accepted by them as worship) and some to Jesus. It was not surprising, then, that one of the saints gave a pointed prophetic utterance saying that God didn't like sharing worship with anyone or anything else, and that we were to express our worship exclusively to God. The honor of worship belongs to God alone, and He will share this honor with none!

A handful of incense upon the coals every time the priest entered was God's minimum, for God's instruction to Moses was, "a perpetual incense before the Lord throughout your generations" (Exodus 30:8). God has chosen that there never be a time when worship is not being offered up before Him.

Where did these coals come from? Since God had kindled the original fire upon the Brazen Altar in the outer court He insisted that all fire used in the ceremonies of the tabernacle come from the Brazen Altar. God has specified, "And he shall take a censer full of burning coals of fire from off the altar before the Lord, and his hands full of sweet incense beaten small, and bring it within the veil: and he shall put the incense upon the fire before the Lord, that the cloud of the incense may cover the mercy seat that is upon the testimony, that he die not" (Leviticus 16:12, 13). The coals came from the altar of sacrifice indicating that the sweet spices had to be combined with the costly sacrifice before they became a cloud of incense. Has anyone yet calculated the price God paid at Calvary, our Brazen Altar in the New Testament?

Worship does, indeed, have a price tag on it. It requires fresh coals that must be produced in the fire that burns on the altar of sacrifice. In order to keep the coals hot enough to ignite the blended spices that comprise our worship incense, we must continue to offer unto God the sacrifices of praise, Bible study, meditation on the things of God, obedience to the will and Word of God, and faithfulness in Christian service. When a Christian's ardor grows cold no amount of spices will produce the incense of worship. We are challenged, "seeing ye have purified your souls in obeying the truth through the Spirit unto unfeigned love of the brethren, see that ye love one another with a pure heart fervently" (1 Peter 1:22), and the Greek word for "fervently" means red-hot. So unsavory is a lukewarm condition that God told the church at Laodicea, "So then because thou art lukewarm, and neither cold nor hot, I will spue thee out of my mouth" (Revelation 3:16). Worship will extract the price of maintaining a fire on the altar of sacrifice and a willingness to bring coals from that fire to the Golden Altar in our soul.

Has worship always had a price attached to it? The very first time that the word *worship* occurs in our Bible it has a very high price tag attached to it, for it is the occasion when God asked Abraham to offer his son, Isaac, as a burnt sacrifice. Abraham told his servants to await him while, "I and the lad will go yonder and worship" (Genesis 22:5). Abraham was prepared to pay the price of losing the son for whom he had waited many years, and for whom there could be no hope of replacement. That God provided a substitute at the very last possible moment does not detract from the fact that in Abraham's soul-spirit he had already paid the price demanded to worship the Lord his God.

Is Abraham the last saint who has been asked to lay his all on the altar in order to worship? Ask the missionaries who serve around the world. Ask the Christian businessmen who plow their profits into gospel ministry, and check with the prayer warriors who give up their recreation hours to bow before the Lord in humble prayer. Fundamentally, it is impossible to worship without paying a price. David knew this implicitly.

So serious was the crisis in David's life and administration that the Bible gives us a full account of this season in his life both in 2 Samuel 24 and 1 Chronicles 21. In spite of God's prohibition, David had grievously sinned in numbering the people; so God had withdrawn His blessing and had replaced it with severe chastisement that was destroying people throughout the land. When God responded to David's repentance David was commanded to offer sacrifices in a specific manner in a specified place. However, the place God had chosen for this worship was already in use by its owner, Ornan, who was threshing wheat. David could not build an altar in the midst of the threshing operation; one or the other had to cease.

While this was being discussed, God allowed Ornan to see the destroying angel of the Lord standing with his drawn sword, and Ornan immediately offered to give the threshing floor to David for whatever atoning sacrifices could be offered. As a matter of fact, he also offered his oxen for the sacrifice and his threshing implements for the wood. Perhaps nothing inspires devotion more rapidly than the prospect of divine destruction.

At this point, David had to come to grips with whether God wanted *him*, the one who had sinned, to offer sacrifices, or whether it would be sufficient merely to have the sacrifices offered. Was it the sacrifice or the sacrificer that God was interested in? Ornan's offer gave David an excellent opportunity to reconcile self-interest with godliness, prudence with principle; of doing a good thing for nothing, for had David accepted the offer the offering would have lacked nothing that God had required as to place, manner, or sacrifice. The command would have been satisfied, and Ornan's offer was both expedient and inexpensive!

But worship must proceed out of the lives of the worshippers. These lives are already occupied with busy schedules that keep our minds and spirits threshing constantly. How tempting it is to let the pastor and church staff do the worshipping for us.

David resisted the temptation of doing a thing the least expensive way and insisted on purchasing both the floor and all the field around it. David felt that it was unworthy of his position and ability as king to freeload in worshipping God. He sensed that it would demean the greatness of God and his own relation and obligation to Him to offer God sacrifices that had cost David nothing. It was a costly transaction, but David valued his religion more than his wealth, so he paid full price for the place. He knew that if he accepted Ornan's offer it would have been Ornan's sacrifice, and that this would not have been an expression of David's spirit, for David was a giver and a true worshipper of God.

How easy it is to fall into the temptation of merely attending a worship service rather than paying the price to be a worshipper. To listen to the musicians play worshipfully is so much easier than to keep in practice on our own instrument so that we can participate. It is less costly to say the "amen" to a prayer than to actually be prayed-up before a service begins, just as it is easier to listen to a choir than to invest the hours necessary to be a participant with a praising choir. Ornan's offer is very pleasing to our flesh.

Real worship begins and is maintained at the cost of much thought, feeling, involvement, and prayer. If a person's prime feeling is of himself, he will take the easiest and most economical way to worship. But if a man's prime feeling is of God, he will pay whatever price is necessary to worship Him fully. In the first case, the person will seek the largest possible results from the least possible expenditure, while in the second case the expenditure will itself be an act of worship. Perhaps in worship there are two fundamental questions: How little *may* we do and how much *can* we do?

David paid the price to worship and offered sacrifices unto God, both burnt offerings, which were typical of the consecration of the worshipper's body, soul and spirit, and peace offerings, which were expressive of reconciliation and fellowship with God. We are told that divine fire came down upon the sacrifices and the judgment of God was stayed. So sacred was this acceptance of his worship that David designated this as the site for the future temple.

David summarized the whole of his attitude towards worshipping God when he responded to Ornan's offer of the free use of the threshing floor for the sacrifice with, "Nay; but I will surely buy it of thee at a price: neither will I offer burnt offerings unto the Lord my God of that which doth cost me nothing" (2 Samuel 24:24). Do we dare offer as worship that in which we have no investment?

Empty hearts, prayerless spirits, tired bodies, undisciplined minds, unopened Bibles, and careless attitudes have ruined far more worship services than all the demonic activity of hell. Satan is not our greatest hindrance to a true and full worship experience; we are our own greatest enemy when we seek to worship without having to pay a price. Still, even persons who would never consider attending a wedding shower or reception without a costly gift will consistently attend a worship service empty-handed. They have not come to give; they have come to receive, but worship is a two-way communication.

If the price of the performance of worship seems unduly high, just wait until we come into the realized presence of a Holy God in our worship experience. We will discover that holiness is not only the characteristic aspect of God's nature, but it is demanded of all who approach their Holy God. Worship and holiness are so closely interconnected that it is impossible to separate them.

CHAPTER 15

HOLINESS AND WORSHIP

Between God's promise to a shepherd lad and David's actual accession to the throne were years of struggle. Even after he was crowned king there were many enemy armies that had to be subdued before his kingdom was secure. Once this was behind him, David turned his attention to bringing the Ark, the symbol of God's presence, back to Jerusalem. When the Ark of the Covenant was finally resting in the tent that David had pitched for it, David handed Asaph, the chief musician, a psalm that had been written especially for this occasion. In the heart of this song David has scored, "Give unto the Lord the glory due unto his name . . . *worship the Lord in the beauty of holiness*" (1 Chronicles 16:29, italics added). This plea is repeated at least twice in the Psalms (29:2, 96:9) as the writers realized that a holy God must be worshipped in holiness and that this holiness, far from being fearsome and dreadful, was beautiful, glorious, excellent, and honorable, as the Hebrew word for "beauty" (*hadarah*) would suggest.

There are at least three aspects of this imperative that the Spirit expressed through David and others. First, the One who is worshipped is holy. Second, the channel through which we worship is holy. Third, the worshipper must become holy in order to be involved in true worship.

That we have been called to worship a holy God is self-evident. Not only is God holy, but only God is absolutely holy; all other holiness is derivative. Some theologians define holiness as the pervading moral attribute of God's nature. Others insist that it is not one attribute among the other attributes, but that it is the innermost reality to which all other attributes are related. God is more holy than He is anything else. Whenever we get a glimpse into heaven and hear the mighty angelic beings praising God it is always "holy, holy, holy" that they chant, not "omnipotent" or "omniscient." The holiness of God is the consummate perfection, purity, and absolute sanctity of His nature. Hence we recognize that God is entirely separate from all that is evil and all that defiles, both in Himself and in relation to all His creatures. There is absolutely nothing unholy in Him at all; consequently there is nothing within Him that can be sympathetic with defilement and sin.

Others have defined holiness as "otherwiseness," that is, holiness is what we are not. It is the nature that God breathed into Adam that made him so completely different or "otherwise" from the rest of God's creation. God is so distinctly "otherwise" that we are hard-pressed to even find similes in life to help us describe Him. After the miraculous deliverance at the Red Sea Moses sang, "Who is like unto thee O Lord, among the gods? Who is like thee, glorious in holiness, fearful in praises, doing wonders?" (Exodus 15:11), and Hannah prayed, "There is none holy as the Lord: for there is none beside thee: neither is there any rock like our God" (1 Samuel 2:2).

Not only is God holy, the channel that enables us to worship God is called the Holy Spirit. In writing to the young church in Thessalonica Paul said, "For this is the will of God, even your sanctification . . . . For God hath not called us unto uncleanness, but unto holiness. He therefore that despiseth, despiseth not man, but God, who hath also given unto us his Holy Spirit" (1 Thessalonians 4:3, 7, 8). Paul clearly coupled God's call to holiness with the gift of the Holy Spirit, for while God has imputed His righteousness to the obedient ones and Jesus has conferred His justification upon the repentant ones, it is the Holy Spirit who has implanted His holiness in the consecrated ones by making His personal abode in their spirits. The Holy Spirit is the channel whereby God's holiness can be made available to us, and He is also the channel whereby we may worship a Holy God, as we have already seen in a preceding chapter.

It is the third aspect of the challenge to "worship the Lord in the beauty of holiness" that often raises barriers to our worship. A worshipper must become holy to continue worshipping a holy God, for holiness and unholiness cannot fellowship together, since one of the prime manifestations of holiness is a hatred of sin. When we approach worship, then, we have a holy God on one extreme and unholy men on the other. Unless God's Son had purchased holiness for men at Calvary and God's Spirit was effecting that holiness day by day in their lives, none of us could worship God.

As I wrote in my book, *Let Us Be Holy,*

"This matter of being holy, then, is far more than a deep religious feeling. It radically affects our life style. It is concerned with our attitudes, actions, associations, adorations, thoughts, love, and obedience level. Holiness is a governing principle of life to be manifested in every area of life as displayed inwardly and outwardly towards God, ourself, or others." (Page 87)

True worship is tremendously demanding upon holiness! The nominal Christian seems almost to get by merely adding God to his former way of life; but the Spirit-filled Christian finds that many of the old actions and attitudes have to be released in order to walk in the Spirit. Beyond this, the praising saint experiences inner workings of the Spirit that cleanse and change motives as well as manifestations. But the worshipping saint never comes to the end of these dealings of the Holy Spirit that change the person from a self-centeredness to a God-centeredness, for Christ did not come to repair, but to replace. He came to trade His life for ours; to bring our lives to the cross so that He can share His life from the resurrection side of the tomb.

The closer one gets to God the greater are the demands for godliness in the individual's life, for God is a holy God who cannot fellowship with or accept the unholy. He can and will share His holiness with anyone who strongly desires fellowship with Him, since God passionately yearns to have this kind of communion with man. He had it with Adam until sin separated the two of them, and he had it with Christ Jesus during the days He was here on the earth. Now, God desires to have it with the Christians of this twentieth century.

In a very real way, holiness is a divine energy that is completely destructive to all that is unholy. It is similar to light (another descriptive aspect of God's essential nature) which, whenever the two meet, cannot help but destroy darkness. Light can join light and actually intensify the measure of light, but light cannot join darkness. Just so, the holiness of God automatically destroys its opposite. The cry, "holiness, without which no man shall see the Lord" (Hebrews 12:14) is less a command and more a declaration of cause and effect.

When one attempts to approach God without holiness He mercifully hides Himself from the seeker, lest if the seeker should come into the divine presence, the holiness of God's inherent nature becomes a destructive laser beam to that worshipper.

Inasmuch as the ultimate level of worship is intimate fellowship with God, it is expected that we must rise to the nature of God before He and we can enjoy such a relationship. While God condescends in grace to redeem us, He expects us to ascend in holiness to worship Him.

I do not mean to imply that one must become absolutely holy in order to have a worship experience with God, for the Bible abounds with illustrations of unholy men worshipping a holy God when His presence was made manifest. Balaam is a classic example of this. But I am saying that holiness is an absolute prerequisite in order to become a consistent worshipper. God invokes worship in the unholy in order to expose them to divine holiness, for until we have seen something of God's holiness we don't even know what true holiness is, nor are we motivated to pay the price necessary to have that holiness effected within us. Since God alone is the source of holiness, and only His Spirit can produce it in the life of a believer, there must be that initial confrontation with God to get the process started.

Holiness, however, is not intended to make life uncomfortable and unnatural. Actually, the opposite is true. Holy living involves life at its fullest, for true holiness brings us into a love, joy, and peace such as this world cannot know aside from Christ Jesus. This impartation makes worship possible at higher and higher levels, for it is a sharing of the very divine nature of God Himself.

The level to which our worship can rise is dependent upon at least two fundamental principles. The first is our concepts of God, which we have already examined earlier in the book, and the second is the level of holiness to which we have attained. We must know Him as He has revealed Himself in the Word, and we must become similar to that revelation.

In my recent book *Let Us Get Together* I remind us that,
. . . life can only truly fellowship life of the same kind. A dog fellowships a dog, and a frog fellowships a frog, but it would be a stretch of the metaphor to suggest that a dog could fellowship a frog. (Page 90)

Along this pattern, God can only truly fellowship that which has His nature and His likeness; that's why He created man in His own image and likeness. That sin has marred man's similarity to God is well demonstrated, but the cross of Jesus Christ has provided restoration of man to the spiritual nature of God, thereby enabling men and women to rise to higher levels of association and companionship with Almighty God. Worship is the outpouring of a soul at rest in the presence of God, and this requires being a partaker of the divine nature.

When Isaiah was caught into the heavens and saw God sitting upon a throne high and lifted up and heard the seraphim chanting the holiness of God, he became totally involved with himself, crying out, "Woe is me! for I am undone; because I am a man of unclean lips, and I dwell in the midst of a people of unclean lips: for mine eyes have seen the King, the Lord of hosts" (Isaiah 6:5). It was not until after one of the seraphim purged his sin with a coal from off the altar that Isaiah could get involved with God. Isaiah's unholiness had to be replaced with God's holiness before he could worship God in any meaningful measure at all, and so must ours.

Since worship is the occupation of the heart, not with its needs or even its blessings, but with God Himself, the heart must be fixed fearlessly upon God and not be torn between introspection and devotion. All concept of self must be abandoned whether it be of self-negation or self-needs, so that the whole of our being can flow out to God in adoration, consecration, and affection. A.P. Gibbs, in his book *Worship* says, "Worship is the overflow of a grateful heart, under a sense of Divine favor." This requires such a measure of God's holy nature as to enable us to be relaxed in the presence of God, otherwise we will be so occupied with our unholiness that we cannot respond lovingly to His holiness. It is, obviously, impossible to be self-centered and to worship God. We must be God-conscious, not self-conscious, to be a true worshipper. Therefore the more God's nature is coursing through us, the greater our awareness of God will be and the less time we will spend involved with ourselves when we approach the throne of God.

In speaking of the Greek word that the New Testament writers used for "holiness", Dr. James Hastings, a scholar of the past century, wrote in *A Dictionary of the Bible:*

> *Hagios* is, above all things, a qualitative and ethical term. It refers chiefly to character, and lays emphasis upon the demands that that which is sacred in the highest sense makes upon conduct . . . . *Hagios* expresses something higher than sacred; higher than outwardly associated with God; higher than reverent, pious, worthy, honourable, pure, or even free from defilement. *Hagios* is more positive, more comprehensive, more elevated, more purely ethical and spiritual.

It is characteristically Godlikeness, and in the
Christian system Godlikeness signifies complete-
ness of life. (v. 2, p. 399)

Godlikeness, then, is a prerequisite to worship, but
how much like God must we become before we can be
worshippers? Perhaps a clue to this can be found in
Zechariah's strange vision where the prophet saw
". . . Joshua the high priest standing before the angel of
the Lord . . ." (Zechariah 3:1). The amazing part of the
vision is the fact that ". . . Joshua was clothed with filthy
garments, and stood before the angel" (Zechariah 3:3).
No high priest would knowingly come into the Holy of
Holies defiled. Before entering he bathed, put on special
garments, washed his hands, face, and feet at the laver
and came in carrying a basin of blood from the brazen
altar and a censer of incense from the golden altar. But,
like Joshua in the vision, even after we believer-priests
have done everything that the Word requires to be
cleansed, when we stand before the ineffable presence of
our holy God we realize that compared to Him we are still
defiled and polluted.

It is noteworthy, though, that this high priest was not
condemned for wearing defiled garments; the angel of
the Lord, an Old Testament manifestation of Jesus, said:

Take away the filthy garments from him. And
unto him he said, Behold, I have caused thine
iniquity to pass from thee, and I will clothe thee
with change of raiment. (Zechariah 3:4)

This priest was not condemned; he was changed! That
which was unholy was removed and replaced with one of
Christ's garments of righteousness. Then the Lord said,
"Let them set a fair mitre upon his head" (Zechariah 3:5).

The mitre, a ceremonial hat that the high priest wore in the holy place, had an inscription on it that read, HOLINESS UNTO THE LORD. Although the priest had done everything he could do ceremonially to be holy, it did not measure up to the holiness of God, so God merely shared His holiness with the priest. So He does with believer-priests today. It is His pleasure to share His nature with those who will come into His presence with as much purity as their faith can appropriate.

God has always been and will always be incomparable in His holiness. His holiness cannot be fashioned in anything that man can see, but whenever God's holiness is made available to man, whether in ritual or reality, cleanness is an integral part, for the removal of unholiness is a prerequisite to the reception of His holiness.

Inasmuch as holiness brings us back into a right relationship with God, it also brings us back into a joyful relationship with life which is the fountainhead of praise and worship, but while both have their source in holiness, each flows in a different stream down the mountain.

Some ten years ago, when I wrote the book *Let Us Praise*, I consistently interchanged the words "praise" and "worship" for, at that level of my walk with God, I accepted them as synonymous terms. During the intervening years I have observed that the Scriptures do not interchange these words, but rather teach that praise prepares us for worship, or that praise is a prelude to worship. Psalm 95 is a good example of this principle. It begins:

O come, let us sing unto the Lord: let us make a joyful noise to the rock of our salvation. Let us come before his presence with thanksgiving, and make a joyful noise unto him with psalms. (verses 1, 2)

That this is praise none would dispute. It is joyful, melodious, demonstrated, and declared praise directed to God. But it is only *after* this praise has been fully expressed unto God that the Psalmist invites us:

O come, let us worship and bow down: let us kneel before the Lord our maker. (verse 6)

The order is praise first, worship second. The same pattern is found in Psalm 96 where we are reminded:

> For the Lord is great, and greatly to be praised:
> he is to be feared above all gods. Give unto the
> Lord, O ye kindreds of the people, give unto the
> Lord . . . the glory due unto his name: bring an
> offering, and come into his courts. (verses 4, 7, 8)

It is only after clearly orchestrating the form of praise that was to be offered unto God that the inspired writer added: "O worship the Lord in the beauty of holiness: fear before Him, all the earth" (verse 9). So while worship may be dependent upon praise, praise is not a substitute for worship; it is, however, a blessed supplement to it.

We Christians use a triunity of terms to describe our responses to God: prayer, praise, and worship, and we often place one word for the other as though they were merely different expressions for the same action. Prayer is usually understood as being concerned with our *needs*, praise is concerned with our *blessings*, while worship is concerned with *God Himself*. This is not to say that prayer cannot be an avenue of expressing worship or that praise will not be concerned with God, but, generally speaking, this is the pattern that they take.

While I am aware that there are at least eight forms or levels of prayer, the most common prayer Christians of this generation pray is the prayer of petition. This is both scriptural and practical, but petition is not worship. Some persons who think that they are worshipping have merely joined the worshippers as petitioners.

In seeking to differentiate between praise and worship, I see at least six areas of contrast that extend from the stimulus behind them to the mode of their utterance. Praise and worship will differ somewhat in their motivation, in their thrust, in their source of inspiration, in their depth of dedication, in their proximity to God, and even in their method of expression.

Since God is more interested in *why* we do than in *what* we do, our motivations are vital. Generally we praise out of a motivation to be blessed of God. We come, not as a petitioner with a need, but as a praiser with a desire for an emotional lift. In praying prayers of entreaty, we request something from God in acknowledgment of our deep need and utter dependence upon Him; in praise we approach God joyfully and enthusiastically to savour to the fullest the pleasure of His presence; but in worship we present something *to* God as a loving recognition and expression of our deep appreciation of what God is and for all that He has done.

Far too frequently what seems to start out as a motivation to worship God quickly degenerates into a lusting to receive something from Him. But the key to worship is to give, not to get. True worship gives glory to the Lord; it does not seek to get glory from the Lord. A worshipper comes to God not to be blessed but to bless; not to enter God's presence as an asker but as an admirer. Praisers who aspire to be worshippers need to ask themselves if they are praising to give unto God or to get from God. In praising are we ministering unto God or seeking ministry from God?

Beyond this contrast in motivation between praise and worship is the diversity in the thrust of praise and worship. The frontal attack of praise is a positive response Godward, based far more upon His deeds than on His person. Repeatedly the Psalmists urge us to praise the Lord for the *things* He has *done.* Moses wrote the song of praise extolling God's dramatic rescue of Israel through the Red Sea; Hannah sang praises to God for giving Samuel to her after a long period of childlessness; and Psalm 107 three times exhorts us, "Oh that men would praise the Lord for his goodness, and for his wonderful works to the children of men!" (verses 8, 21, 31).

This thrust of praise is prescribed, proper, and very profitable, and it is certainly a step beyond thanksgiving; but it is, admittedly concerned far more with what God has done for us than with who God actually is. Praise tends to be more concerned with God's *presents* than with God's *presence*.

Because praise is act-centered, it often becomes petition in a positive form, or is an attempt to manipulate God to grant us present desires by greatly praising Him for His past gifts to us. It is possible for us to come before the presence of the Lord and to perform proper praise with a motivation to get, not to give, and never go beyond praise into worship. Actually, at those times, we have stepped backward from praise to prayer instead of forward from praise to worship.

In contrast to praise, worship's main thrust is toward the God who has done these great things. While the injunction to praise is often followed by the word "for," the command to worship points to a Person. "Worship God;" "worship the Lord;" and "worship Jesus" are all scriptural commands. Praise begins by applauding God's power, but it often brings us close enough to God that worship can respond to God's presence. While the energy of praise is toward what God does, the energy of worship is toward who God is. The first is concerned with God's performance, while the second is occupied with God's personage. The thrust of worship, therefore, is higher than the thrust of praise.

Still another disparity between praise and worship can be found in the source of their inspiration. Fundamentally, praise is an exuberance in the human soul/spirit that is expressed to God, while worship flows from God's Spirit who is resident in the spirit of man. Praise is redeemed men calling to God, while worship is God calling to God from within redeemed men. Praise often has its origins in the soul, but true worship will always originate in the spirit, for just as Jesus told the woman at the well, "God is a Spirit: and they that worship him must worship him in spirit and in truth" (John 4:24).

All divisions between soul and spirit are of necessity arbitrary and tend to be more theological than practical. Still, we recognize the difference between emotional inspiration and spirit inspiration in our responses to God. Praise is more apt to be an act of emotion while worship is an act of devotion. Praise springs from the fountain of our feelings, while worship flows from the spring of our spirit. Praise says, "I feel . . . ." Worship says, "I love." Praise looks to the hand of God; worship looks to His heart. While praise and worship are very much alike, they flow from separate sources in our being even though each must manifest itself through the same body. The manifestation does not always reveal the source, for both praise and worship can be expressed with the same bodily postures or actions.

A fourth difference between praise and worship may be found in the depth of dedication evidenced in the praiser as contrasted to the worshipper, for while praise is an expression of our life, worship is a life-style. The prophet even speaks of Christ giving us ". . . the garment of praise for the spirit of heaviness . . ." (Isaiah 61:3), but nowhere does the Bible speak of worship as a gift from God or something that can be put on as a garment.

Praise is often an act of our will, and it can be stirred into action by the working of our emotions, but worship involves the entire life. A true worshipper is a worshipper whether he is engaged in an act of worship at the moment or not. Worship is far more than an attitude or an action, it is a way of life that affects the worshipper's behavior outside the presence of God as well as inside that presence. You can tell a true worshipper by his actions on the job, his attitudes in the home, as well as his ardor at church. His time with God changes him in all of his relationships in life.

Rev. Charlotte Baker, founder and pastor emeritus of King's Temple in Seattle, Washington has been a long-time pioneer of the message of worship throughout the world. In a recent conference where we shared together she stated, *"Worship is extreme submission and extravagant love."* This demands a life-style, for submission is a long-term commitment. We do not have a "season" of submission as we so often have a "season" of praise. Praise may be as brief a period as a moment, or it may last for an hour or more, but submission to God is for a lifetime, and if worship is "extreme submission" then the worshipper is called upon to be extremely submitted to God throughout the whole of his life.

If worship is also "extravagant love" then surely it is more than an attitude or a mere act. It will take a lifetime to extravagantly love God. Jesus taught us, "thou shalt love the Lord thy God with all thy heart, and with all thy soul, and with all thy mind, and with all thy strength: this is the first commandment" (Mark 12:30), and obedience to this level of expressed love will become a lifetime occupation that produces a life-style in the worshipper.

Daniel is a classic example of these two forces at work in the life of a worshipper. Although captured as a youth and taken to a foreign land, Daniel accepted this as the will of God for his life. In the midst of the most perverse circumstances we can imagine, he continued to pour out his love unto God. Even when the edict of the king made it life-threatening to do so, Daniel continued his thrice daily worship response to God. His life was so surrendered to God that he simply refused to do things the king's way if it conflicted with God's revealed will. Yet his spirit remained loving toward God in the midst of all the pressure. Whether in training, in service, or in the lion's den, Daniel was a worshipper, for it was a way of life for him. His life was one of extreme submission to God and extravagant love poured out unto God.

Praise may be a style of expressing life, but worship is a life-style in itself. In praise we express a deep appreciation to God for the things He has done for us, but in worship "we live unto the Lord" (Romans 14:8).

Still a fifth difference between praise and worship has to do with our proximity to God. Praise, admittedly, is not always concerned with the deeds of God; it sometimes looks beyond what has been done and praises the one who did it, but it is usually a response from a distance. As we will point out in the next chapter, praise is the vehicle of expression that brings us into God's presence, but worship is what we do once we gain an entrance to that presence. Praise can be done from a great distance, but worship, before it can flow, requires being in the presence of God. In the Tabernacle in the wilderness, praise was practiced even before they entered the outer court, but worship was confined to the holy place; it required an intimacy not needed for praise.

Praise and worship make a good marriage in the sense of being lifetime partners. We find them linked together repeatedly in the pages of the Scripture, for while praise prepares the believer for worship, it is worship that fulfills praise by lifting the expression of praise from appreciation to adoration and by directing its focus to a person rather than to His exploits.

It is hopeless to try to divorce praise from worship, for they are an eternal team. They work together like a hand and a glove. For instance, to be a true worshipper, whatever we do must be a response to an interaction between our spirit and God's Spirit, not as an interaction between us and the persons in the pews around us. But when we come to church we do not walk into the presence of God, we walk into the presence of people and our initial action will be influenced by those people. We'll join them in singing and in various rituals of the service, and in the midst of this we will often be inspired to praise. Although the initial praise may primarily be an interchange with the ones around us, it often lifts us to a one-on-one encounter with God which, in turn, opens the door for the needed response between our spirit and God's Spirit which produces worship.

In this case, praise was the bridge between earthly function and heavenly unction. We praised ourselves out of the pews into God's presence so that worship could flow unto God. Praise can flow with people, but worship is totally concerned with God!

A final diversity between praise and worship might be the method of expression they use. Each must be expressed through the channel of our bodies so, quite obviously, there will be many similarities between them, but a trained observer will also see great dissimilarities.

For instance, praise is very vocal while worship is often void of much speaking. Some declare that praise is the vocal end of worship, and while there is some truth in that statement, it bypasses the very real possibility and common reality of praising without ever worshipping. Two lovers on a walk have much to talk about, but when they are locked in an embrace words seem superfluous.

So it is, often, in worship.

Praise is often physically demonstrative with great action, while deep worship is far more likely to be physically submissive than physically active. We might say that praise tends to be emotional while worship is devotional, and that praise is often loudly exuberant while worship is more apt to be quietly exultant.

Would we better understand this contrast if we said that praise puts love into words and action while worship puts love into touch and relationship? Each is important, but worship is higher and the more intimate.

We cannot by-pass praise or negate it, for it is the route into worship. The musical channel for the release of praise is perhaps the most gentle route into worship that God has given to us. But we do not desire to remain in praise when God's presence makes worship a distinct possibility.

17

LEADING OTHERS INTO WORSHIP

That the hundredth Psalm is the divine pattern for entering into the presence of God is obvious to even the most casual reader. Too frequently, however, we begin the pattern at verse four instead of at verses one and two. Long before we "enter into his gates with thanksgiving" we are instructed to "make a joyful noise . . . come before his presence with singing" (verses 1, 2).

The Hebrews would have no difficulty understanding this, for they were accustomed to singing on their journey to Jerusalem for the feast days, and they even ceremonially sang the psalms of ascent, or degrees (Psalms 120 to 134), as they approached the holy city for these festivals. Their singing reviewed the purpose of their visit, stirred their faith in the Lord their God, and united their hearts and minds with those of their fellow pilgrims.

These psalms of degrees start with man's need—"In my distress I cried unto the Lord . . ." (Psalm 120:1)—and end in God's sanctuary with men blessing God (Psalm 134:2). From man's need to God's presence is quite a walk; perhaps that is why they sang fifteen songs.

It is likely that the concept of a song service comes from this Jewish practice, but it has been degraded in some religious circles. Sometimes the song service is little more than a call to order, while on occasions it is used to fill time as latecomers find seating in the church.

Scripturally, singing is provided as an expression of worship that can lift us out of the pressures of life into the presence of God. But this is not automatic, for while singing can unite our hearts in a bond of faith and a united expression of love, it can also sidetrack an entire service and immobilize the best of worship desires.

Just as there is a great difference between getting a mass of people to walk aimlessly down a street and leading a band in a march, so singing can either get people involved in aimless activity or lead them to a specific goal. The first will afford emotional release and some soulish responses, but the second can lead people into the presence of God and a worship experience.

Almost anyone can lead songs, but it takes someone special to be able to lead *people* as they sing. This person must be a worshipper himself if he is to lead others into worship, and he must know where he is, where he is going, and when he arrives.

Leading people always requires beginning where the people are. The song leader must locate their present spiritual position or he will miss them entirely, for few people will run to catch up once the march has begun. In most church services, locating the level of the people will generally be easy, for people have come to church from the activities of normal life and have a very minimum of God-consciousness. Their minds are concerned with people, places, things, and personal needs. They are very self-conscious.

The song leader might well start with a song or chorus of personal experience or testimony—one of the many "I am" or "I have" musical testimonies. This meets the people where they are and gives them something with which to identify early in the service.

In the typology of the Tabernacle in the wilderness, to which this hundreth Psalm alludes, this would be the encampment immediately outside the fence that surrounded the Tabernacle. It was the home of the priests, who, although encamped close to the Tabernacle, could not worship until they had entered the Tabernacle itself. And neither can we. If the song leader will bear in mind that songs about personal condition or experience are songs to be sung when the people are outside the Tabernacle enclosure, he can make excellent use of them to gently get the attention of the singers.

Since the Scripturally-declared purpose of gathering together is to worship, the goal of every song service should be to bring people into a worship experience. That would occur in the holy place, where the illumination of the Holy Spirit (the candlestick) makes fellowship with God (the table of shewbread) and worship of God (the altar of incense) possible, pleasurable, and profitable. We want to bring the singers into the holy place where they are conscious of this; but as it is more than one step from outside the court to inside the holy place, songs of experience should not be immediately followed by songs of God's greatness.

"Enter into his gates with thanksgiving . . ." (Psalm 100:4), the Psalmist instructs. Don't leave the people in the priestly encampment all the time; take gentle, progressive steps to move them closer to God's presence. This psalm lists three or four such steps, and *thanksgiving* is the first. Let the congregation enjoy singing songs of testimony until they are sufficiently united to begin moving closer to God. Use such songs to move the people through the gate that will separate them from the profane into the sacred, and then introduce songs and choruses of thanksgiving.

It is a matter of bringing them from a consciousness of what has been done in and for them (testimony) to Who did it in and for them (thanksgiving). The procession through the eastern gate into the outer court should be a joyful march, for thanks should never be expressed mournfully or negatively. While the people are singing choruses of thanksgiving, they will be thinking both of themselves and of their God, but by putting the emphasis upon the giving of thanks, the majority of the thought patterns should be on their God. Singing at this level will often invoke a beginning level of praise, but it will not produce worship, for the singers are not yet close enough to God's presence to express a worship response.

Step number two is "enter . . . into his courts with praise" (Psalm 100:4). Once the heart has been lifted in thanksgiving, it is natural for it to take the progressive steps into praise. To thank God for what He has done evokes praise for Who he is, so move the songs from thanksgiving for past favors to praises for His present mercy. The outer court is a fairly large place, so it may require more time singing choruses and songs of praise to move the people toward the holy place than it required to get them through the gates with music of thanksgiving.

Progressing from one step to another may require a few words of transition, but the leader whose goal is to bring people into the worship of God will weigh his words carefully. Many a praise service has been talked to death by an anxious song leader, since a long "commercial" breaks the thought patterns of the singers. A well-prepared leader can say what needs to be said in a paragraph or less.

The closer we get to the presence of God in the Holy of

Holies, the more the songs will be concerned with God Himself. "Be thankful unto him, and bless his name," the Psalmist says (Psalm 100:4). Whereas we started singing about ourselves outside the walls, we will end up singing about God inside the holy place, for nothing in there speaks of man; it is in its every aspect a revelation of God. Here is where some of the majestic hymns give expression of higher concepts of God than do some of the simple choruses, but if it is a chorus-oriented congregation, let the choruses be those which direct all of the attention to God, Jesus, or the Holy Spirit.

If the leader has been successful in bringing the people step by step into the outer court and on through it into the holy place, there will be a rise in the spiritual response of the people. Instead of mere soulish, emotional responses, there will be responses from the human spirit that have depth and devotion in them. The emotional clapping will likely be replaced with devotional responses of upturned faces, raised hands, tears, and even a subtle change in the timbre of the voices. When there is an awareness that we have come into the presence of God, we step out of lightness into sobriety.

It is at this point that too many leaders make a serious mistake by jerking the people back into the outer court with an emotional chorus of thanksgiving. Worship takes time; don't rush the people. Let them sing; let them repeat any chorus or verse of a hymn that seems to give honest expression to what they are feeling and doing at the moment. The mind can jump from one concept to another far faster than the spirit can. Allow the spirit to savor the sense of the presence of the Lord. A change of chorus can destroy the entire worship attitude.

Just worship. Cleverness is inappropriate. Talk is unnecessary. Directions for response are superfluous.

Let the people worship. Silence may be threatening to the leader, but it is golden to the worshipper. A gentle, sustained chord on the organ and a song of the Spirit on the lips of the leader should be more than sufficient to carry a worship response of the entire congregation for a protracted period of time.

"But that isn't singing," you say.

Of course not. It is the purpose of singing. The saints are worshipping; that's why we lead the singing. Don't let the tool of singing hinder the worship response. Everything we have done has been for this, so stop doing, and let the worship flow throughout the congregation. When the majority seem to have finished their worship, the whole congregation can either be invited to sit down "in His presence," or you may choose one more chorus to lead them back to the outer court for the preaching of the Word or whatever other ministry has been prepared.

Singing should not be considered an end in itself. It should be a release of the Holy Spirit unto God in a worship expression. But people have to be led from the natural to the spiritual and from expression of self-needs to an expression of spirit-worship. This is the task of the song leader. If he succeeds, he will be a leader of worshippers more than a leader of songs.

Of course, singing should not be considered as an end in itself, for our purpose in assembling together is to worship the Lord in the beauty of holiness. Worship is the end; all other activities, ceremonies, or ordinances merely serve as a means to that end. But while worship is the end for all of our means, it, of itself, is a means for transforming our individual lives, for a worshipper cannot help being changed in the midst of his worshipping.

18 TRANSFORMATION AND WORSHIP

Man is uniquely a religious creature. His intellectual superiority over all other animals is undisputed, and he is very aware that he is the zenith of all creation. Surely his supremacy is not because he evolved to a higher level than anything else, but it is because he was created in a different manner than anything else.

The Genesis account declares that God created the earth and all of its inhabitants with His word: ". . . God said, Let there be . . ." (Genesis 1:3). But of the creation of man we read, ". . . God said, Let us make man in our image, after our likeness . . ." (Genesis 1:26). Man was created by the hand of God, not merely the word of God. Furthermore, God created man from His own image, formed him into God's own likeness, and "breathed into his nostrils the breath of life; and man became a living soul" (Genesis 2:7). Man, far more than any other living thing, is a specific and special creation of God.

In addition to this, man was created for a very special purpose. Paul succinctly stated it in saying, ". . . we should be to the praise of his glory" (Ephesians 1:12). Man was unquestionably created a religious creature, for there is in the very nature of man something which causes him to recognize and worship a superior being. Whether this "something" is an inner instinct or the effect of tradition, descending from the first worshippers, through all the tribes of the human family, man is indeed a religious being.

Never in all the explorations men have made throughout the earth has a tribe of men been discovered who did not recognize the existence of a superior being and worship it in one way or another. Man worships something which he believes to be endowed with the attributes of a superior being. It has often been said that man has a God-shaped vacuum within his spirit which produces a universal reaching out to worship a superior being.

But while man is a worshipping being, he needs guidance in the choice of the object of his worship. For man, by worshipping, becomes assimilated into the moral character of the object which he worships as the standard of perfection. Accordingly, then, he condemns everything in himself which is unlike, and approves of everything in himself which is like, that character. This causes him to abandon everything in the course of his life which is condemned by the character and precepts of his god, and to conform himself to that standard which is approved by his god. Obviously the worshipper wants the favor of the object he worships, and he reasons that it can only be obtained by conformity to the will and character of that object. To become conformed to the image of the object worshipped must be the end desire of the worshipper. These very aspirations cause his character to become more and more like his god.

The history of idolatry gives ample proof of this. Consistently the character of every nation and tribe throughout the history of civilization has been molded and shaped by the character attributed to their gods. Indeed, man becomes like the object of his worship.

The early Egyptians illustrate this. These patrons of

the arts and sciences were brute-worshippers, having their sacred bull, ram, heifer and goat. Historians report that bestiality, the lowest vice to which human nature can descend, was common at that time. The Egyptian sculpture and paintings reveal that the minds of the worshippers were filled with debased, vile and unnatural desires.

Another example of the power of idolatry to change men into the character of the gods they worshipped is that of the Scythians, who finally overthrew Rome. Their chief deities were ideas of hero-kings, bloodthirsty and cruel. Therefore, the worshippers possessed a horrid delight in reveling in slaughter, mayhem and blood. Since they believed that one of their hero-gods, after massacring much of the human race, destroyed himself, it was considered ignoble to die a natural death. Those who were not killed in battle frequently committed suicide, fearing that a serene death might exclude them from favor in Valhalla. Like god, like people.

Better known to most of us is the example of the goddess Venus, called Aphrodite by the Greeks. Although referred to in literature as the goddess of love, as worshipped by the nations of antiquity she was actually a personification of lust. Acts of worship done in her honor would be "X-rated" in today's society. In Paul's day in the beautiful city of Corinth, whose temple to Venus was world-renowned, the persons who were considered to be the most sacred in the city were prostitutes, consecrated to the worship of Venus. This was the major source of revenue for the temple. Consequently, the inhabitants of Corinth became proverbial for dissoluteness and debauchery.

From the beginning of civilization to the present day, men have clothed depraved or bestial deities with almighty power. They became cruel, or corrupt—bestial in their affections—by the reaction of the character worshipped upon the character of the worshipper. In the words of an anonymous writer, "They clothed beasts and depraved beings with the attributes of almightiness, and in effect they worshipped almighty beasts and devils."

This premise is not only recognized by Christians looking at idolatry from the outside, but was admitted by some of the most brilliant minds in the midst of the corruption. Plato speaks of the pernicious influence of the conduct attributed to the gods and suggests that such histories should not be rehearsed in public, lest they should influence the youth to commit the same evil. Aristotle advised that statues and paintings of the gods should exclude all indecent scenes, except in the sacred temples, which presided over sensuality.

H. Oakley, Esq., a magistrate in Bengal, India, some years ago, was quoted as saying, concerning the worship of Kali, one of India's most popular idols, "The murderer, the robber, and the prostitute, all aim to propitiate a being whose worship is obscenity and without imploring whose aid, no act of wickedness is committed. The worship of Kali must harden the hearts of her followers; and to them scenes of blood and crime must become familiar."

Writing of the latter years of Rome and Greece, the moral Seneca exclaimed: "How great now is the madness of men! They lisp the most abominable prayers, and if a man is found listening they are silent. What a man ought not to hear, they do not blush to relate to the gods." He goes on to say, "If any one considers what things they do, and to what things they subject themselves, instead of decency he will find indencency; instead of the honorable, the unworthy; instead of the rational, the insane."

Such was heathenism and its influence, in its most enlightened ages, according to the testimony of the best men of those times. These men, as men of today, were indeed religious creatures who became conformed to the moral character of the object they worshipped.

But does the Scripture support this thesis? The Psalmist declares, in the picture language of Hebrew: "Their idols are silver and gold, the work of men's hands. They have mouths, but they speak not: they have ears, but they hear not: noses have they, but they smell not: feet have they, but they walk not: neither speak they through their throat. They that make them are like unto them; so is every one that trusteth in them" (Psalm 115:4-8).

The Hebrews to whom this was written recognized that far more than the construction of idols was being discussed. Not only did man fashion the visible representation of their god, but they formed the concepts that were projected to that deity. Their god was a god of their craftsmanship, of their concepts, and of their imagination. And having formed their gods, they became like them.

The first chapter of Romans bears further testimony to this: "And changed the glory of the incorruptible God into an image made like to corruptible man, and to birds, and four-footed beasts, and creeping things. Wherefore God also gave them up to uncleanness through the lusts of their own hearts, to dishonour their own bodies . . ." (Romans 1:23, 24).

Whenever man projects the attributes of deity to his own creation and then worships it, whether it be a visible idol, a myth, or a mental concept, he risks becoming exactly like his creation: first, because the worshipper has formed something of his own image; second, because the worship is soon assimilated into the moral character of the object of his worship; and third, because ". . . God gave them up unto vile affections" (Romans 1:26).

But as dismal as this principle is when applied to idolatry, it becomes an exciting provision when seen from the Christian perspective.

Paul exhorted the saints at Colossi: "If ye then be risen with Christ, seek those things which are above . . . . Set your affections on things above . . ." (Colossians 3:1, 2). For since the worshipper takes on the character of the worshipped he need but worship the true and living God to partake of His character.

"Look up and be changed," Paul was saying.

The New Testament consistently teaches that change in the life of a believer is needful, desirable, and available. It speaks of men having been "darkness" who have now become "light in the Lord" (Ephesians 5:8). It declares, ". . . Such were some of you: but now ye are washed . . . .sanctified . . . justified . . . by the Spirit of our God" (1 Corinthians 6:11). Furthermore, it contrasts the natural works of the flesh with the spiritual fruit of the Spirit (Galatians 5:17-23) and even declares: "[Ye] have put on the new man, which is renewed in knowledge after the image of him that created him . . ." (Colossians 3:10).

Even more pointedly, Paul told the Corinthian church, "But we all, with open face beholding as in a glass the glory of the Lord, are changed into the same image from glory to glory, even as by the Spirit of the Lord" (2 Corinthians 3:18). "Beholding . . . [we] are changed!"

These changes that worship will produce in the worshipper are, then, progressive ("from glory to glory"), imputed ("by the Spirit of the Lord"), and very consistent with what occupies the attention of the worshipper ("are changed into the same image").

But what seems to be overlooked, frequently, is that he is changed only while "beholding the glory of the Lord."

In the setting of the Old Testament Tabernacle we could say that we are not changed appreciably in the outer court where the ministry of the brazen altar and the laver are attended to; it is in the holy place where God's glory is seen as a Shekinah that character changes are effected. It is in the awe of worship that we are altered in our ways.

This is not a crisis experience but a continuing one, "from glory to glory." It is while we are beholding that we are becoming like Him. The adorer is adjusted to whatever level of glory he can see, and this level becomes the platform from which increasingly greater levels of glory may be viewed. Little by little, from faith to faith (2 Corinthians 10:15) and from strength to strength (Psalm 138:3) the Holy Spirit changes us from our depraved character to God's divine character—"even as by the Spirit of the Lord." It is not instantaneous nor are there any short cuts, but there also are no failures, only dropouts.

The rate of change is controlled by the worshipper. The more he worships, the more he is changed. Daily sessions in the divine presence will produce daily assimilation into God's character, while mere sporadic seasons of worship will produce only erratic changes. It is not the capriciousness of God's will but the constancy of man's worship that determines the rate of spiritual maturation.

Since the object of our love determines the character of our life, and the intensity and regularity of the expression of that love will determine the rate at which we are changed, we can understand why Christ declared that the greatest commandment of God's Word is, "Thou shalt love the Lord thy God with all thy heart, and with all thy soul, and with all thy mind, and with all thy strength" (Mark 12:30), for the character of the worshipper will always be assimilated into the character of the object of his worship.

God's special creation may have been marred and scarred by sin, but it can be regenerated and animated by bringing it into the presence of its Creator as surely as the dried seed can be brought to life by placing it back into the earth from which it came. Man, the religious creature, can be restored to God's image only when he is in God's presence, and worship is the prescribed avenue for entrance into that transforming presence. "Beholding . . . we are changed."

If the need for change is so apparent, and if the channel for that change is worshipping God on a consistent basis, would we not expect God, who alone can effect these needed changes, to bring back to this world a revival of worship?

REVIVAL AND WORSHIP

I was raised with the concept of revival. My heritage had its beginnings in such an outpouring of the Holy Spirit as to raise up a people whose hearts hungered after God. One of the methods they used to promote church growth was the conducting of "revival services," which usually consisted of a guest speaker, special music, and services every night for two to six weeks. As the years passed by, the church grew, and as the world seemed to turn upside down, these revival services often became more "rival services" where one church tried to outdo a sister church across town. Other times the announcement of a "revival" conjured up visions of survival as the people remembered how this evangelist forcefully preached on "hellfire and brimstone." It was not always easy to get a commitment from the members of the congregation to support such a revival and, through the years, these revivals gave way to other emphases.

For some years in my early ministry I carried a negative attitude toward "revival." I saw it as an Old Testament word, and pointed out that we never need to revive that which is alive and functioning, so the church should never need to be revived. Furthermore, I was convinced that the closer we would get to the end of time, the greater would be the falling away of the saints. I had a devil who was too large, a God who was too small, and a church that was too weak. About the only hope I could hold out to the saints was a secret rapture at some moment when the devil was preoccupied.

What confidence God has in His Church to let individuals of such limited and perverted vision take leadership. Fortunately, God is going to do what He has purposed to do in spite of what His preachers do or say. No amount of preaching about apostasy and falling away is going to keep God from renewing His work in the Church of the last days. We may talk survival, but God is purposing revival. We may expect failure in the Church of the twentieth century, but God intends to expedite success beyond our wildest imagination. The Psalmist was a better visionary than many of us, for he cried, "Wilt thou not revive us again: that thy people may rejoice in thee?" (Psalm 85:6).

All students of church history are aware that there have been great revivals in days past, but "wilt thou not revive us again?" We have just come through a twenty-year cycle of the renewing of the work of the Holy Spirit in the churches of America and in the true Church of the Living God, but "wilt thou not revive us again?" Is Jehovah a God of the past or is He a God of eternity? Did He not reveal Himself as the I AM and then proclaim "Jesus Christ the same yesterday, and to day and for ever" (Hebrews 13:8)? What God has done, He is doing, and whatever He is doing, He shall still do, for there is a continuum in God that cannot be violated.

All through the Old Testament, whatever God set out to accomplish was done with finality. He led His people into the Promised Land almost against their will— certainly in spite of their repeated murmurings—and gave them every piece of territory that they would occupy. No change in the economy and no change in leadership kept God from making His people glorious and holy in His sight. God said that He would take them in, and He did.

Why, then, do we worry about recession, cartels, changes in world leadership, and ungodliness? Can they stop God from presenting to this world a Church which is glorious, spotless, and full of the power of God? America's philosophy of humanism and the rights of the individual has not hindered God's express plan for revealing His Son through the Church; if all the power of Rome could not prevent the birth, and hinder the revelation, of Jesus, certainly there is no political or ideological power on earth today with sufficient strength to even slow down God's program of purifying unto Himself a people who can be presented to His Son as a bride and to this earth as the very Body of Christ. Paul was "confident of this very thing, that he which hath begun a good work in you will perform it until the day of Jesus Christ . . ." (Philippians 1:6). God never starts something that He cannot complete; He started reviving His church, so we have a right to expect Him to continue reviving her until she is ready for presentation to Christ and to the world.

That the early Church was pure, powerful, and productive is revealed in the Book of Acts, but through the years that followed, religious men, for various reasons and using varied methods, defiled the purity of the Church, depleted her power, and decimated her productivity. That which had been birthed as a living organism was reduced to a lethargic organization. The rule of the Holy Spirit was supplanted by human spirits in the persons of the clergy. The divinely prescribed approach to God was replaced with an elaborate man-made labyrinth so complex that even the priests could not find the presence of God. The marvelous approach to God as revealed in the tabernacle in the wilderness seemed lost to the Church forever.

The early Church brought the light of revelation to the world, but the enchained Church contributed to the Dark Ages. As in Samuel's days, the light of the Lord was just about extinguished. Although the system was corrupt, some of the men in that system were concerned and genuinely hungry for God. Among them was Martin Luther, whose heart cry reached out to God until God revealed to him the truth that ". . . the just shall live by his faith" (Habakkuk 2:4). This was echoed by the Apostle Paul, "The just shall live by faith" (Rom. 1:17).

Justified by faith, not by fiat! It was revolutionary in Luther's day. His teaching of the Pauline doctrine that it is not by works of righteousness but by God's grace alone that men stand justified before God caused him to be viewed as a radical and a heretic. But God was restoring the brazen altar to the Church through a fresh emphasis on the cross of Christ Jesus. Martin Luther's teaching of justification by grace on God's part and by faith on man's part returned to the Church the realization that we have been completely pardoned from the penalty of sin. God chose to place all the punishment for sin upon His Son at Calvary. As Paul put it, "Christ was without sin, but for our sake God made him share our sin in order that we, in union with him, might share the righteousness of God" (2 Corinthians 5:21, TEV). This double imputation, whereby God imputed our sins to Christ on the cross and also imputed His righteousness to us in return, formed the backbone of the revelation given to Martin Luther. Once again men could begin their approach to God, for the issue of the guilt of sin was adequately handled by God and needed only to be faithfully embraced by men.

Just as Israel's approach to God began with the substitutionary sacrifice of an innocent animal at the brazen altar that stood in the outer court just inside the eastern gate, so our approach to God must begin at God's brazen altar, the cross, where the innocent victim died as a substitute for the sinful person. Until sin's penalty is completely satisfied we dare not approach God, the righteous Judge of all the earth (see Genesis 18:25; Hebrews 12:23). Because of the cross we are now both guiltless and blameless; therefore, we can "draw near with a true heart in full assurance of faith, having our hearts sprinkled from an evil conscience . . ." (Hebrews 10:22). This is the message of justification. This was the ministry Martin Luther shared, and thousands of people joined him until, ultimately, the great Lutheran denomination was founded to continue to promulgate the great truth that the cross has never lost its power.

For 250 years this was *the* game in town; it was the revolutionary message of the dynamic Church. Then, in the mid-eighteenth century God began to move dramatically in the lives of two brothers by the names of John and Charles Wesley, inspiring them to see the truth of sanctification throughout the Scriptures. They had long embraced justification, but they were unsatisfied with the continued presence of sin in their lives even after they had experienced God's forgiveness. Charles Wesley preached that there was a place in God where not only was sin's penalty revoked, but sin's pollution was removed. He was not content to be assured of escape from the flames of an eternal hell; he wanted present deliverance from the fire of sin's inner habitation. He embraced the injunctions of Scripture to "likewise reckon ye also yourselves to be dead indeed unto sin . . . . Let not sin therefore reign in your mortal body, that ye should obey it in the lusts thereof. Neither yield ye your members as instruments of unrighteousness unto sin . . . for sin shall not have dominion over you" (Romans 6:11-14).

Whether he was completely aware of it or not, Wesley was used of the Holy Spirit to return the laver to the service of the Church. The laver, the second piece of furniture in the outer court, was made of the mirrors of the women and was kept filled with water. It was used by the priests for the cleaning of their hands, faces, and feet before going into the holy place to minister unto the Lord, for the Lord had threatened death to any priest who dared to enter the holy place defiled. The laver offered a place of both self-inspection and self-purification, for the same basin that revealed defilement afforded the means to remove that contamination. This is the image behind Paul's testimony of Christ's love for the Church when he wrote, "that he might sanctify and cleanse it with the washing of water by the word" (Ephesians 5:26). Those who would minister exclusively to people may get by with little more than justification, but those who aspire to minister unto the Lord must also submit themselves to the sanctifying power of the Word of God.

With the return of the truth of sanctification, the Church had a twofold message: pardon from the penalty of sin (justification) and purification from the pollution of sin (sanctification). These messages that brought men into the outer court of God's presence were without significant addition for the next 150 years. Wesleyism produced the great Methodist movement and became a denomination with world-wide influence.

It wasn't until the early twentieth century that another major revelation of God was shared with the Church on earth. It began with a world-wide outpouring of the Holy

Spirit that was misunderstood, maligned, and misinterpreted by the mainline denominations. Those who got involved in this new thing were often disciplined out of their churches, and through their need for fellowship a new religious organization came on the scene. This early Pentecostal outpouring brought the believers beyond the outer court relationship with God into the holy place. They went beyond the hanging of "Jesus the Way" and dared to enter the doorway marked "Jesus the Truth." God used them to focus the attention of the Church upon Christ the Golden Candlestick. These early Pentecostals had an amazing perception of the Redeemer from sin. God imparted great illumination and revelation to them, and although their experience was the infilling of the Holy Spirit, their message was *Jesus*. So notably did they preach Jesus that many of the fundamental denominations labeled them heretics because they rarely used the name of God—everything was "Jesus." In light of this fresh illumination of Christ they were very evangelistic in nature and missionary-oriented in ministry. They founded churches everywhere, and they sent missionaries to the four corners of the world. They did not emphasize the mere work of Christ; they had caught a glimpse of the Redeemer and they wanted everyone else to see Him "as He is."

The faith, enthusiasm, and inspiration of these who had gone into the holy place became infectious, and before long these Pentecostals were growing faster than any other church body. Their Christ-centered singing, testifying, and preaching reached over the wall to affect even those who had originally rigidly rejected them. With the aid of better transportation and rapid communication, they were able to reach the world with their message in a mere fraction of the time it took to promulgate the truths of justification and sanctification. In contrast to the 250 years between Luther and Wesley and the 150 years between Wesley and the early Pentecostal outpouring, this re-establishment of the lampstand was the "new message" for only 50 years before the next major revival swept the world.

With the ministry of the brazen altar (the cross), the laver (the Word), and the golden candlestick (the person of Christ) well established in the true Church, it was time for the Church to come into fellowship with itself. For too long different segments of the Church had fearfully and suspiciously stood aloof from one another. But a divided body is a defenseless body. So in another outpouring of His Holy Spirit, God brought into being the Charismatics, whose main contribution to the Church has been partnership with the redeemed. Their conventions were billed as "Holy Spirit conventions," but the main ministry was feasting together in spiritual fellowship. This move brought the Church to the golden table of shewbread around which the Old Testament priests met weekly for feasting and fellowship.

In the Charismatic revival, God caused His people to step beyond their doctrinal boundaries and to be united partakers of the spiritual life and strength that is in Christ Jesus. While this revival did not bring new doctrine to the Body, it brought a renewal of the ministry of the cross and the Word with a fresh appreciation of Christ and His many brothers and sisters in this great Body, the Church. Perhaps its greatest contribution was in making the believers aware of the many similarities that exist among us in spite of the differences that have separated us for so long. We have found that as long as we are feasting upon the shewbread (also called "the bread of His presence") we have a common basis for fellowship with one another. It has taught us "how good and how pleasant it is for brethren to dwell together in unity" (Psalm 133:1).

Some have pronounced the Charismatic renewal as the final revival God has promised before the return of Jesus, but I have grave reservations about this. First of all, there is still one piece of tabernacle furniture that has not yet been returned to the Church: we are missing the golden altar of incense where continual worship was offered up to God. Every time a priest entered the holy place he was commanded to take a handful of incense and to scatter it over the hot coals on this golden altar. This cloud of incense smoke permeated the atmosphere of both the holy place of the priests and the most holy place, which was God's habitation among men. Furthermore, it saturated the skin, hair, and clothing of the priests, causing them to bear the fragrance of the knowledge of God with them to the needy people in the outer court.

By the grace of God the Church has come back to pardon from the penalty of sin, purification from the pollution of sin, a fresh perception of the Redeemer from sin, and into a partnership with the redeemed from sin, but she has not yet experienced much participation with God Himself. Although each revival has brought a renewal of praise, there is a true dearth of pure worship in the Body of Christ today. We can praise our way into His presence, but generally we do not know what to do once we gain admittance to Him.

None who know the ways of God could be comfortable with the statement that "this is the final revival." Certainly God would not return only four pieces of furniture to the Church when it required five stations (five is the number of grace) to allow the Levitical priests entrance to God. God, Who has begun a good work, will complete it. If the new wine that Christ produced for the wedding at Cana of Galilee was better than the old wine, should we not expect that the final provision will greatly exceed the first provision? The glory of the Church's inception will be greatly exceeded in the Church's final hours. The power, victory, growth, influence, ministry, and worship of the Church seen in the Book of Acts will be signally surpassed in the coming revival that will bring the Church back to such an intimate relationship with the Father that she will instinctively know how to worship and will distinctively want to worship.

The best is yet to come! I believe that I can prove this from the Word. I know that God has spoken it to my heart, and I can bring the testimony of many, many people who declare that God has equally quickened to them that there is a move of God in the wings just awaiting its cue before coming to center stage. God has told me that it would begin in America and Australia almost simultaneously and would work together and spread across the world in very rapid fashion.

He told me that the nature of the move would be a fresh revelation of God the Father. In the Pentecostal revival there was an unusual revelation of Jesus, and in the Charismatic revival we experienced a supplementary revelation of the Holy Spirit, but our generation has not had a wholesome unveiling of the Fatherhood of God. As a natural outgrowth of this unique presentation of God the Father, worship will spring forth, for throughout the Scriptures, every person who came into an awareness of God immediately worshipped Him.

Since, as we have learned, worship is a response to a *person*, it will require such a revelation of God the Father in order to produce world-wide worship in the Church; but God has promised it, history requires it, and our experiences long for it.

When will it happen? I don't know. Between Luther and Wesley was a span of 250 years. Between Methodism and Pentecostalism was 150 years, but only 50 years separated the Pentecostal revival from the Charismatic renewal. At that ratio, we might expect the next revival "yesterday," for the Charismatic renewal is already 25 years old!

We do not have the dates revealed, but we do know something of the times and seasons. Revival is closer than we may think. Worship will be the theme of that revival, and already some segments of God's Church have entered into this glorious experience. Fortunately none of us need await the forthcoming revival to enter into worship, for that is available to us right here and now.